Violence and Oppression

Violence and Oppression

James C. Dick

The University of Georgia Press
Athens

Copyright © 1979 by the University of Georgia Press
Athens 30602

All rights reserved

Set in 11 on 14 point Linotype Baskerville
Printed in the United States of America

Library of Congress Cataloging in Publication Data

Dick, James C.
    Violence and oppression.
    Bibliography.
    Includes index.
    1. Violence—United States.   2. Oppression Psy-
chology.   3. Government, Resistance to.   I. Title.
HN90.V5D5   301.6'33   78-2235
                ISBN 0-8203-0446-8

To the memory of Cliff Kaufman

Contents

† Preface

Historians have suggested that "the study of violence itself is not a particularly important pursuit." Understanding collective action is important, but collective action results in violence only if resisted by the authorities, "and resistance can be adventitious and contingent."[1]

However, the premise of this study is that whereas violence is often a peripheral part of a larger process of collective action and social change, there is moral and social significance in crossing the line leading to violence. This is true even of violence to property—only those who haven't worked to build and construct are likely to watch its destruction with unalloyed glee. It is surely true of violence to persons. Even premature death from natural causes is not easy for the survivors to come to grips with, and the difficulties are compounded when the loss can be attributed to human agents. Even if from the standpoint of a historical or social understanding killing seems inevitable and epiphenomenal, from the standpoint of the individual agent who deals out death an important moral choice has to be made. The men and women whose actions are considered in these pages did not take up the gun without some deliberation. They made decisions of moral import, and it would be demeaning and disrespectful to belittle or ignore their capacity for acting responsibly.

An attitude of respectfulness toward these actors also suggests the importance of exploring how violence as well as the much more frequently discussed phenomenon of civil disobedience can be justified. The problem of civil disobedience deserves a preeminent place in political theory because of its relation to the understanding of the nature of political obligation. Nevertheless, from the perspective of the individual actor the decision to disobey is not so weighty or agonizing as the decision to destroy and kill. Recurrently throughout history even the most humble actors upon the political stage have faced a dilemma as to whether to join their fellows in an uprising bent on killing or to avoid the onus of responsibility for the taking of human life. It is a difficult dilemma worthy of exploration.

The precise character of the dilemma can best be understood by an analysis steeped in the actualities of history. Its terms are after all set by historical fact and circumstance, so any theoretical analysis can only mislead if it is not properly connected to such facts and circumstances. One way to prevent the elision or misrepresentation of the exigencies and peculiarities of history is to base one's analysis directly on them, and that is what I have attempted here.

In my efforts I have acquired many debts that can be repaid only in gratitude and its manifestations. I am indebted to Lou Lipsitz for asking questions that I was hard-put to answer and, most of all, to JoAnn, without whom this book wouldn't have been the same, and not just because she typed the entire manuscript.

Violence and Oppression

Introduction

About violence there is one certainty: it does harm and wreaks damage. It may do some good as well, but this is no certainty. When, despite these verities, are the victims of oppression justified in resorting to deadly violence? That is the topic of this book. This topic is narrow. It concerns not violence in general, but only violence of a certain type, of a certain scope, and from a certain source.

Not all harmful or destructive acts are violent. Demolishing an old hotel or slapping an hysterical patient cannot fairly be called violent acts. Those acts are violent that exceed certain bounds of normality and propriety. Where these bounds lie varies from time to time and place to place, as social needs and the way of life in which they fit vary.[1] But the norms that define violence are not purely subjective or culturally variant. "The fact that men are about equally concerned with and susceptible to injury and pain . . . probably gives the words 'violent' and 'cruelty' a relatively stable core of application in spite of their logical characteristics."[2]

The type of violence considered here is but a small part of this stable core of the application of the general concept of violence: physical harm to—indeed, the actual killing of—human beings. And the scope of this sort of violence as discussed here is rather narrowly delineated. No outbreaks of homicidal violence that result in more than a few dozen fatalities are considered. Murderous jacqueries and millenarian outbursts of medieval times as well as the slaughter of thousands in Cambodia, Colombia, Guatemala, Indonesia, and Biafra in recent years are obviously phenomena of a moral and social order different from those discussed in the following pages. My assumption is that such phenomena are also less plausibly justifiable than the actions I consider.

Violence may differ not only in type and scope, but also in source. Both private citizens and agents of the state may engage in violent acts. As it happens, the sanctity of human life is more often violated by agents of the state than by private citizens. The normal pattern in the history of modern Europe[3] and in many cases of violence on the part of the underdog in the United States has been for the crowd to aim its destructive efforts at property. The response of the police or militia has often been to shoot to kill so as to oblige the crowd to disperse. As a result the kill-ratio between police and protesters is often highly favorable to the former. In the riots in the black ghettos during 1964–68, the most recent large-scale crowd violence in America, this pattern reasserted itself as the rioters spent most of their energy on looting and arson and the police and militia, on assuring that three or four times as many blacks as peace officers were killed.

Quite possibly it is out of prudential and expedient considerations that private citizens have been more restrained in the taking of human life than peace officers have. But this disparity means nonetheless that ignoring the taking of life by private citizens, that is, excluding from consideration the violence of those who have position and power, leaves out a great deal. For, as Richard Hofstadter has observed of the course of American history, in most of those instances when violence "appears to have served its pur-

pose . . . it has been, on the whole, the violence of those
who already had position and power."[4] The peculiarly
American phenomenon of vigilantism, for instance, was
usually organized and directed by the more affluent members of the community, and in labor disputes employers
were much more likely to use deadly force, and use it successfully, than were strikers.

When violence of this type, scope, and source is described, we find acts that are not only of great moral weight
and seriousness, but are also plausibly justifiable. But this
plausibility is heightened, again despite the essential character of violence, when it is further stipulated that the
agents of violence may truly be said to be oppressed.

What does it mean to be oppressed? What characterizes
the agents of violence whose deeds are scrutinized in these
pages? To oppress, the *Oxford English Dictionary* tells us,
is "to affect with a feeling of pressure, constraint, or distress; to lie heavy upon, weigh down, burden, crush (the
feelings, mind, spirits, etc.) [and] to trample down or keep
under by wrongful exercise of authority of superior power
or strength; to load or burden with cruel or unjust im-
positions or restraints; to tyrannize over." This definition
has both a subjective element (to feel) and an objective one
(to be). I emphasize that I am concerned only with the
objective condition of oppression; the mere subjective feeling of oppression cannot by itself serve to justify violence.
In chapter 3 a more precise meaning is assigned the condition of oppression, but notice now that it is a condition
that immediately renders somewhat plausible the notion
that homicides committed by those suffering under it ought
not be classified as murders. We may plausibly conclude
that they ought not to be because two wrongs can sometimes make a right.

Violence is a wrong. It is not "eufunctional" behavior. The very idea of violence makes it "conceptually impossible to value, or even to universally prescribe, . . . other than as a means to an end." It cannot *coherently* be considered valuable in itself. The command to do whatever is considered violent implies seeking a condition in which violence is the norm. But if violence has ceased to be a relatively rare occurrence, the events in question would be considered not violent but routine. The correct application of the adjective *violent* entails that the conduct to which it refers is aberrant and unusual. That killing and injuring almost universally are regarded as being violent is attributable not to the logical characteristics of the word *violence,* but rather to the contingent fact that such actions' becoming the norm is incompatible with social cohesion, or, in other words, to the universality of certain human needs and interests.[5] It follows that violence can be justified only by appealing to some offsetting good that it results in, since taken by itself it is merely harmful and aberrant.

Even Frantz Fanon's grandiose claims for the virtue of violence can be assimilated to this scheme. Fanon asserts that "At the level of individuals, violence is a cleansing force. It frees the native from his inferiority complex and from his despair and inaction; it makes him fearless and restores his self-respect." This assertion is empirically false, since other forms of militant and effective action may serve as a psychological restorative, and the doing of violence may be inconsistent with a sense of self-respect if one has not descended into a state of brutishness. People of moral sensitivity, as Kai Nielsen remarks, in extraordinary circumstances may plant bombs to kill the innocent and yet not exhibit a corrupt mind. But if they do not do so "with evident heaviness of heart"—and Fanon seems to suggest that they should rather exult in what they are doing—that fact in itself might be enough to convict them of fanaticism and corruption and of being an enemy of the people.[6] Although the empirical premise of Fanon's argument is false, if it *were* true, then the psychologically restorative power of violence would serve as the offsetting good that a defense of the inherent evil of violence requires. Fanon contends that the psychological benefits of violence to those who make use of it are sufficiently great to offset the evil inherent in the harm that it does.

Since violence is justifiable only as a means to an end, plainly any plausible defense requires that the violence to be defended be capable of serving some good end. The stipulation that the violence be directed at the removal of the burden of a cruel or unjust imposition or restraint supplies the good end that a justification of violence requires. Whereas it is wholly implausible that pointless murder or the taking of life for an unworthy purpose may be defensible, it is a plausible and interesting proposition that violence and even the taking of life when directed at the removal of oppression can in some circumstances be justified. Although it might possibly be argued that *oppression* is a term of hyperbole with little application to the condition of part of the population of the citizenry of a democratic state, it is clear that unless this term or some other equally strong one is applicable, no defense of the violation of the sanctity of life could possibly get very far. To see whether in fact it does have application is part of the purpose of the historical exploration in chapter 1.

I want to emphasize that justifying violence is my concern, and not merely excusing it. The distinction, as drawn with exemplary clarity by J. L. Austin, is this. We begin with a situation in which someone is accused of having done something that is somehow or other untoward, and thereupon he or someone else on his behalf tried "to defend his conduct or to get him out of it. One way of going about this is to admit flatly that he, X, did do that very thing, A, but to argue that it was a good thing, or the right and sensible thing, or a permissible thing to do, either in general or at least in the special circumstances of the occasion. To take this line is to *justify* the action, to give reasons for doing it: not to say, to brazen it out, to glory in it, or the like." Justification of the taking of life by the oppressed is the topic of this essay.

Justification stands in contrast to a different way of going about defending the accused person's conduct or getting him out of it, which is to admit that it wasn't a good thing to have done, but to argue that it is not quite fair or correct to say baldly, "X did A." We may claim that it isn't fair just to say "X did it"; perhaps he was under somebody's influence or was nudged. Or it isn't fair to say baldly, "he did A"; it may have been partly accidental, or an unintentional slip. Or it isn't fair to say "he did simply A—he was really doing something quite different and A was only incidental, or he was looking at the whole thing quite differently." Naturally these arguments can be combined or overlap each other. As Austin summarizes the distinction: "In the one defense . . . we accept responsibility but deny that it was bad: in the other, we admit that it was bad but don't accept full, or even any, responsibility."[7]

Now if a people are truly oppressed, excuses for their violence should abound simply by reason of the fact that they are oppressed. Deprived of education, they are likely to be ignorant of whatever alternatives to violence do exist and hence are unable to take advantage of them. They may be naive about the probable effects of their violence, or driven by uncontrollable emotions, or they may misperceive the oppressor's intentions and misunderstand his actions and take stronger action than the facts justify.

Excuses abound, but it is better not to assimilate all instances of violence that we might wish to defend to this category, partly because, as Austin remarks, "few excuses get us out of it *completely*: the average excuse, in a poor situation, gets us only out of the fire into the frying pan."[8] But still more because merely excusing the violence of the oppressed may rob them of the dignity that is their due. What Allan Silver has observed of the ghetto riots has a general application:

Negro urban violence has already produced spokesmen—not only visible ideologues but anonymous rioters briefly quoted in the Kerner report itself—whose definitions of Negro rioting affirm it as a positive and voluntary act. . . . Much would be lost—humanly, politically, and from the viewpoint of social science—if official interpretive ideology functions to elide or ignore Negro definitions of riot as purposeful, affirmative, and actively chosen. Men who engage in dangerous and desperate behavior—indeed, any behavior—have a certain claim to have taken seriously the meanings which they see in their own acts, and wish others to see in them.[9]

We owe those who run the risks of violence the minimal respect of taking their assertions of responsibility seriously. Then too, those cases where reasoned justifications can be put forward—those cases where the actor is prepared to brazen it out, to glory in it, or the like—are morally more interesting and important than cases where he struggles to get out of the fire and into the frying pan. The attempt to excuse implicitly concedes the indefensibility of the action itself, whereas the attempt at justification brings to the fore the issue of its propriety.

In summary, my concern in these pages is to answer in whole or in part the question as to whether the violation of the sanctity of human life can be justified when it is done by the oppressed or on behalf of the oppressed with a view to lightening or removing the burden of their oppression. In approaching this question I begin with a detailed historical account of four episodes, drawn from American history, in which the oppressed resorted to deadly violence in circumstances that plausibly may be believed to have justified their doing so. These case studies make up chapter 1.

I next consider, in chapter 2, perhaps the most natural defense of the violence of the oppressed, that it may be a justifiable means of bringing about social change. After translating the notion of social change into the language of morality, I find that in none of the historical examples considered did violence serve to bring about a substantial improvement in the conduct of the oppressor, and that it is therefore difficult to justify on this ground. So in chapter 3 I cast about for some more adequate defense of the violence of the oppressed, again understood to be directed not against property but against life.

Chapter 3 begins with an account of the standard legal justifications of homicide. The extent to which they apply to the problem of the justification of the violence of the oppressed is then examined. In chapter 4 the argument of the foregoing chapters is summed up by seeking to explain and establish the validity of five criteria that deadly violence must satisfy if it is to be justifiable.

1
History

A good deal of the murderous violence perpetrated by downtrodden or underprivileged people has been without a shred of justification, or, more precisely, attempts at justification can be easily exploded as rationalizations for barbarism. One such incident took place at Herrin, Illinois, in June of 1922 when, in the midst of a coal strike, some fifty imported strike-breakers, after being surrounded by and surrendering to armed strikers, were told to run and were then shot at. "Some were tied together and shot when they fell, some had their throats slit, some were hanged. In all, nineteen men were murdered."[1] One doubts that such actions would be seriously defended, and even if they were, the arguments put forward against more moderate actions in other situations will serve to prove their indefensibility.

I completely exclude from consideration whole classes of historical violence, such as that directed against the American Indians, on the ground that it was clearly unjustifiable and was perpetrated by the powerful and wealthy against the weak and poor. But it is no doubt true that in certain particular cases (to continue to make use of the example of the Indians) it was whites who were weak and beleaguered and the victims of unjustifiable savagery. For my purposes this does not matter. The general tenor of my remarks is that violence is seldom justifiable—only in quite extraordinary circumstances. Since the examples of violence by the oppressed to which I lend consideration are certainly among the most plausibly justifiable in American history, any strictures against them must necessarily also hold for either less or equally plausible cases.

I limit the extent of my examples of violence to American history. The United States today has as much violence as does any other industrialized society, and its past has on the whole been bloodier than those of most other modern nations. But America has never known certain extreme forms of revolutionary violence (the Parisian *sans-culottes*, the Russian peasantry). Nor has it been witness to any violence even approaching the magnitude of the massacre of the Huguenots following Saint Bartholomew's Night of 1572 in France, the massacres of English and Scotch settlers in the 1641 uprising in Ireland, or, more recently, the slaughter of tens of thousands in Colombia, Indonesia, Bangladesh, and Burundi. In comparison with these catastrophes, every incident I delve into seems virtually trivial. When a few dozen lives are lost, both victims and perpetrators still remain within a social context in which an extremely high value is placed on human life. But when restraints are relaxed to such an extent that tens and even hundreds of thousands of lives are snuffed out in the space of a few months, it seems evident that the very foundations of morality have collapsed and that the most basic of human norms and expectations are in suspense. These are events at the outer bounds of the moral universe, if indeed they do not transpire beyond those bounds. They richly deserve and demand understanding and evaluation, but they are quite beyond the pale of what I consider here.

The four incidents from American history I have culled out for close scrutiny meet all of the criteria set out in the introduction and also involve at least four fatalities for which the oppressed bear responsibility. These killings can be more or less plausibly defended as justified under the circumstances. In my search for incidents that meet these criteria I have relied chiefly on Hofstadter and Wallace's *American Violence: A Documentary History*.[2] Narrowing the field to only four cases has the advantage of permitting detailed examination of each and the disadvantages of rather arbitrarily eliminating from consideration incidents involving only one or two fatalities, of letting a good deal ride on my own perhaps arbitrary judgment of what is plausibly defensible, and of not being based on a really thorough search through the annals of American history for candidate cases. It is my belief that the four cases I have chosen will serve well enough to raise important issues of some general import and that the justifiability of these four cases is not substantially less than that of any other that a more thorough search or a more judicious assessment might discover and select. But if this belief is mistaken, especially in the latter respect, my thesis that deadly violence can be justified only rarely and with difficulty will be undermined.

With this caveat as a preface and a warning, let us turn to the first of the four episodes. My hope is that each episode will serve to illustrate in various ways some general conclusions about the justifiability of violence and that together they will serve to erode, if not to sweep away, the notion that those victimized by oppression may justly victimize by violence in their turn.

The Battle of Alamance

During the revolutionary era of American history three major rebellions pitted the farmers and small merchants of the western regions against a government dominated by the landed gentry and large merchants of the eastern seaboard. (A century earlier, similar conflict had occurred concerning trade with the Indians, the settlement of the frontier, and war against peaceful tribes.)[3] The best known of these rebellions are Shays's Rebellion (Massachusetts, 1786) and the Whiskey Insurrection (Pennsylvania, 1794). But probably the best justified was the "War of the Regulation" in North Carolina, which peaked in 1770 and was suppressed the following year. Shays's followers were members of the debtor class who were being unfairly taxed, dispossessed, and jailed. Their grievances were perhaps as profound as those of the North Carolina Regulators, and like them they finally were driven to shut down the local courts by mob action. But Daniel Shays was not at all anxious to take the lives of any troops sent out against him,[4] and when matters did come to a head in the ill-starred attack on the arsenal at Springfield, Shays's men did not fire a shot before they broke and ran.[5] In this incident there was very little "violence of the oppressed" to be justified or to be condemned. Similarly, in the case of the Whiskey Rebellion the only real battle was an attack on a house guarded by a mere handful of federal soldiers (eleven), none of whom were killed. Moreover, the immediate grievance of the insurrectionists (their being required to stand trial in federal court in Philadelphia, an arduous journey from their homes) had been dealt with by a change in the federal law six weeks before the "battle" occurred.[6]

The grievances of the Regulators went deeper than those of the whiskey insurrectionists; they were somewhat similar to those of Shays and his followers. One complaint the Regulators lodged against the provincial government was that it imposed excessive taxes. This must be a moot point,

even though the poll tax probably did fall with special
weight on residents of the western part of the colony. What
cannot be denied is the injustice of the sheriffs' habit of
coming unexpectedly to a farmer's home, demanding immediate payment in cash, and thereupon proceeding to
seize some property in lieu of payment. As thirty petitioners from Orange and Rowan counties asserted in 1768,
"tho' to Gentlemen Rowling in affluence, a few shillings
per man, may seem triffling yet to Poor people who hast
have their Bed and Bed clothes yea their Wives Petticoats
taken and sold to defray these charges, how Tremendious
judge ye must be the consequences, an only Horse, to raise
Bread or an only cow to give milk to an Helpless family
by which in a great measure are otherwise supported, seized
and sold and kept for a single levy." Injustice was compounded after the seizure of property by vendue sales
rigged to ensure that insiders would get the distrained land
and goods at a fraction of the value.[7]

Whether tax rates were excessive or not perhaps mattered
less since the sheriffs who did the collecting used their authority as much to line their own pockets as to raise revenue
for the public exchequer. The generally accepted estimate
of the amount of embezzlement is that made by the able
and astute governor of North Carolina, William Tryon,
who in 1767 wrote that because local treasurers were afraid
to sue the sheriffs on whom they depended for reelection,
"the sheriffs have embezzled more than one-half of the
public money ordered to be raised and collected by them."
Not surprisingly, one of the foremost of the Regulators'
demands was simply that taxes be "agreeable to Law and
Applied to the purposes therein mentioned."[8]

Probably the most acute grievance of all was that against
the extortionate fees collected by sheriffs, clerks, registers,

and lawyers. Despite legal restraints, overcharging was rife. One frequent device was to break one service into several distinct operations, and charge a fee for each. The whole sorry process was eloquently described in George Sims's "Address to the People of Granville County" written at the onset of the Regulation in 1765. In one historian's paraphrase, Sims

presents as a hypothetical case a man who has had execution levied on him by a merchant for a five pound debt secured by a judgment note [a legal device whereby a creditor could recover without going to trial merely by having a justice of the peace issue execution]. Personal effects to the amount of the judgment are seized, but the poor man's troubles are not over. For entering the judgment on the court docket and issuing the execution—"the work of one long minute"—the justice of the peace demands forty-one shillings and five pence. Unable to pay the fee, the unfortunate debtor is confronted with the alternative of a distraint or twenty-seven days work on the justice's plantation. But even after he has worked out his debt to the justice, the poor man's account is not settled. "Stay, neighbor," says Sims, "you must not go home. You are not half done yet. There is the damned lawyer's mouth to stop. . . . You empowered him to confess that you owed five pounds, and you must pay him thirty shillings for that or else go to work nineteen days for that pickpocket . . . and when that is done you must work as many days for the sheriff for his trouble [in levying execution and selling the debtor's goods], and then you can go home to see your living wrecked and torn to pieces to satisfy your merchant.

Residents of the North Carolina Piedmont in the 1760s must have felt that local government officials had abused their authority to such an extent that they were in actuality more like a band of thieves than a government worthy of respect and obedience. The specific acts of theft to which they objected were further worsened by the political and

economic circumstances in which they occurred. Citizens
of the Piedmont counties were grossly underrepresented
in the provincial assemblies. In the tidewater region, one
representative was returned by between 100 and 150 white
taxables. In Orange County each delegate represented
about 1600 voters.[9] The farmers in the West also were victimized by a scarcity of money in the region, attributable
to the shortsighted financial policy of the provincial government, which too rapidly redeemed currency issued
profligately during the French and Indian War.[10]

In the newly settled lands of the Piedmont, landholders
were frequently obliged to secure the services of lawyers
and take conflicting claims to the government for resolution if they wished to avoid the risk of ejectment. Both
winner and loser paid dearly. The rapacity of the courthouse ring was inescapable. The gravity of these grievances
led Elisha Douglass to conclude (at p. 80) that "it is a won-
der that the Regulator war did not break out sooner and
become more violent than it did."

Violence was slow in coming not because of the ameliora-
tive government action, but rather the willingness of the
Regulators to exhaust every peaceful alternative open to
them before taking up arms. The first tactic tried was petition for redress of grievances. Despite the anguished sense
of injustice felt by the Regulators as expressed in Sims's
"Address," the early petitions to the governor are most
remarkable for their explicit rejection of illegality and
violence and the extreme respect for authority and its perquisites they exhibit. Sims's own address embodied similar
sentiments:

First let us be careful to keep sober that we may do nothing
rashly. Secondly, let us do nothing against the known and
established laws of our land that we may not appear as a fac-

tion endeavoring to subvert the laws and overturn our system of government. Let us behave with circumspection to the Worshipful Court inasmuch as they represent his Majesty's person, we ought to reverence their authority both sacred and inviolable, except they interpose, and then, Gentlemen, the toughest will hold out the longest.[11]

Petitionary campaigns proved ineffective, and by 1768 some Regulators were driven to send "a paper to court officials announcing their refusal to pay taxes until an accounting was reached." But even this angry declaration spoke nothing of taxation without representation or other doctrines questioning the bases of governmental authority, "but merely observed that 'the king requires no money from his subjects but what they are made sensible what use it's for' " and concluded with a plea for a meeting with their assemblymen.[12]

However, attempts to organize tax strikes apparently fell afoul of the power of the sheriff to distrain the property of isolated individual farmers. Regulators did succeed in securing a promise from the governor to let them bring suit against local officials in court, but the fulfillment of this promise brought no relief since the judges, themselves mired in corruption, dismissed the suits or let the offender off with a nominal fine. Ultimately the Regulators took full advantage of their last legal recourse, the political process, and succeeded in returning a pro-Regulation majority to the legislature. This majority managed to pass laws that fixed attorneys' and clerks' fees and imposed penalties for nonobservance, put the chief justice on a salary, renewed an act regulating executions, and eased court costs in litigation over small debts. But the legislature seems to have been more concerned with symbolic gestures than with genuine reform, since all penalties were

civil and contingent on a suit from the injured party. Until
the government took responsibility for marshaling its own
resources to oppose the local officials by prosecuting violations as criminal acts, the farmer was unlikely to receive
justice in unfriendly courts in a suit against his knowledge-
able and powerful adversaries. The fundamental difficulty
was the strong local control by officers so deeply involved in
embezzlement that they would never submit to an accounting, except under compulsion, compounded by the in-
ability or unwillingness of the provincial authority to intervene against its own appointees at the local level.[13]

In a long and still extremely useful account of the Regulator movement written when the colonial records of North
Carolina were first compiled, John Bassett of Trinity College (now Duke University) observed that by the summer
of 1770 the Regulators of Orange County "had become
well-nigh desperate. They had tried petitions to the governor and the assembly, and they had tried the courts.
From neither had they gotten relief." The Superior Court
began its session in Hillsborough, the seat of Orange County, in September. When it convened on the morning of
Monday, September 24 about 150 Regulators crowded into
the room and demanded that officials guilty of peculation
be brought to account. After half an hour of discussion inside the courtroom they went outside to decide their next
move. One of the town's busier lawyers, John Williams,
started to enter the building. The crowd set upon him and
beat him with sticks and leaded whips. They then moved
back into the courtroom, seized Edmund Fanning, the
leader of the courthouse ring, by his ankles and dragged
him down the stairs, bumping his head on each step. He
was then whipped, clubbed, and kicked. The next victim,
a deputy clerk, was knocked down and set upon but was

soon forgotten as an assistant attorney general named William Hooper was dragged and paraded through the streets and treated to the mockery and contempt of his captors and onlookers. Several other gentlemen were whipped; a few managed to flee. Next day Fanning's house was broken into; his papers were burned, his furniture was destroyed, and finally the house was demolished. Fanning, who was put on the street, left town to escape worse treatment. Members of the crowd also broke into several stores and rifled their contents.[14]

This is the worst violence initiated by the Regulators. It was not a pleasant business, but a good deal can be said in mitigation of what was done. We should in fairness first of all remember that, as one student of the conflict observes, "in that day physical punishment was usual; often the legality of the court trials only led to whippings, brandings, and hangings."[15] And in the eyes of the Regulators they were not undermining law and order but rather, in the already emergent vigilante tradition, rendering popular justice because governmental institutions were incapable of doing so. The Regulators' target, however, was the government itself instead of outlaw elements drummed out of the community. As one of the Regulator leaders wrote to a friend two months after the Hillsborough riot, "it was for the sake of public justice that we prosecuted every officer, and not for resentment, spite, malice, nor gain; but the motive that stirred me up, was the repeated cries of the poor, oppressed people. 2dly. It was for the reformation of Magistrates and other Officers that we sued on the penal laws, and not for the sake of the penalty." The Regulators' fundamental objective was the modest and unexceptionable one of withholding their money from support of the government "until we have some probability or assurance

it will be applied toward the support of government."[16]
The lawyers and clerks were guilty; they could not be prosecuted in the courts—so should they not be punished outside the courts in the way accepted at the time?

Naturally the members of the established government
would not view matters in this light. The Regulators' September excursus into violence undoubtedly, as Alonzo
Thomas Dill remarks, "horrified the easterners in North
Carolina and in the tidewater lands of neighboring prov-
inces." Dill even goes so far as to conclude that "the cause
of the Regulators suffered immeasurably by the Hillsborough riots." That is a moot point, since more polite and
restrained tactics were doing little to further the cause. But
the Regulators' impromptu punishment of their oppressors
did prove in the end an exercise in futility. As Bassett as-
sesses the affair:

It turned out they could do nothing but obstruct the court.
The fault lay in the system of government in force in the colony. With such a strongly centralized government, there was
no avenue by which the people had access to reform. The ideas
of government held by the royal agents and their numberless
hangers-on who swooped down on the defenseless colonists
made it impossible that these agents should ever understand
even the point of view of the protesting people. Their action
here can but seem like a mad rush against fate. The people
seem so to have regarded it. . . . [N]ot so many [as three or four]
hundred took part in the proceedings.

After the Hillsborough riots the legislature managed in its
December session to pass a number of reform measures
tightening central control over the conduct of sheriffs and
the fees set by attorneys and officials. It also erected four
new counties so as to increase the number of representatives in the legislature from the west. Possibly "the new

laws might have worked the reform that was necessary to quiet the discontented." [17]

However, the rebellious spirit afoot among some Regulators now made it unlikely the government would display such patience and forbearance. During March a letter from one leading Regulator to another was intercepted. Its writer made claims about the growing strength of the Regulation and also the unwillingness of the local militiamen to fight against it. The writer ended by asserting "that the Regulators are determined to whip everyone that goes to law, or will not pay his just debts, or will not agree to leave his cause to men where disputes [sic]; . . . in short, to stand in defiance, and as to thieves, to drive them out of the country." [18] The government was eager to support its sheriffs in levying taxes due, to enable the courts to meet once again without disruption, and to arrest sixty-two Regulators charged for their role in the Hillsborough riot.[19] Governor Tryon already had these specific objectives in mind when only a month after the riots he expressed his intention to raise the militia "for suppressing these Riots, Collecting the Taxes and bringing the offenders to the Justice of their Country"—in a word, "to extinguish this dangerous flame." [20]

Some Regulators had gone so far as to talk of being "forced to kill all Clerks and Lawyers" and of declaring Fanning an outlaw to be killed on sight. Bassett is clearly correct when he states (p. 198) that "however friendly one may be to the Regulators, he must see in this a movement which the British Government of the time could not allow to proceed." Nevertheless, the goals of the movement remained singularly modest and unexceptionable to the last. The day before the climactic battle between the Regulators and the army led by the governor, the petition presented by the inhabitants of Orange County to Tryon asked no more than to have "roguish officers discarded, and others more honest propagated in their Stead," to see dishonest officials "brought to a clear candid, and impartial Account of their past conduct," and to give voice to other grievances long labored under "without any apparent Hope of Redress." [21]

The governor might have agreed with the substance of these demands, but he felt that he could not tolerate their expression in riot and disruption of the operations of government. His attempt to raise an army to take control of the western counties at first met with little response, but by offering a bounty of forty shillings and good pay during service, Tryon enlisted an army "of the meaner sort." It also included nearly all the gentlemen of prominence from all over the province.[22] On April 23 this army, led by Governor Tryon, left the capital of New Bern near the coast. The army reached Hillsborough on May 9.

As the biographer of the Regulators' best-known leader points out, "The Regulators had [had] more than two months from the announced intention of the Governor to drill and provide themselves with arms. They could have made themselves formidable. But [the Quaker] Herman Husband was not a man to counsel such proceeding," nor apparently were the other men foremost in the movement. The forces arrayed against the governor's army probably numbered twice his one thousand. But if we can accept the estimate of one mid-nineteenth-century historian, only half of them were armed. The Regulator army, as Bassett indicates (p. 202), had other weaknesses as well. "They had neither definite aims nor efficient organization. Their leaders seem to have thought that by making a show of force they would frighten the governor into granting their de-

mands." From Bassett's account (p. 203) it appears that a
good many of the Regulator soldiers did not realize the
seriousness of the situation. Just a few minutes before the
firing began, "the men . . . were engaged in wrestling
matches, when an old soldier who happened among them
advised them to look out for a volley." The armies were
lined up only twenty-five yards from each other "with each
party uttering the most violent imprecations and bandying
the most abusive epithets. The Regulators shook their
clenched hands at the governor and Mr. Fanning and
walked up to the artillery with open bosoms, defying them
to fire." [23]

However, the moment came when Governor Tryon ordered his men to fire. Perhaps because his voice could not
be heard amid the tumult of imprecations, he was not
obeyed. Tryon rose in his stirrups and called out "Fire!
Fire on them or on me!" Fighting quickly became general.
At least some of the Regulators seem to have fought well,
sniping at the governor's troops from behind rocks and
trees, Indian-style. But in the second hour of battle, possibly because of the discipline of the government troops and
their use of artillery, the Regulators were put to rout. Nine
men on each side were killed, and sixty-one loyalists and a
larger number of Regulators were wounded.[24]

In the aftermath of the Battle of Alamance, the fortunes
of the farmers of western North Carolina declined. As Bassett describes the new situation, "The attempt to secure
reform in local government had thus failed most signally.
The people had now either to submit or to move out into
the wilderness again." In the legislature a few bills in line
with the purposes of the movement were passed. But the
offending county officers remained in power and in the
next elections to the legislature, candidates sympathetic to

the Regulators fared badly. In the months following the battle at least fifteen hundred residents of the Piedmont counties, and probably a good many more, departed from their homes and moved farther west. Of those that remained, a significant number were so disaffected that they fought on the side of the Tories during the Revolutionary War that began four years after the battle.[25]

Nat Turner's Slave Revolt

Nat Turner and his band of followers were by far the most bloody-minded and murderous of the four groups of violent men considered in these pages. This incident, the largest American slave revolt to get beyond the planning stage, took place in Virginia, some fifty miles west and a little south of Norfolk in Southampton County, which borders North Carolina. The leader of this revolt, Nat Turner, was born in 1800. A precocious child, he learned to read and write at a young age and apparently discovered from reading and experimenting how to make paper and gunpowder. He became very conversant with the Bible and developed what Eric Foner calls "a religious commitment bordering on fanaticism."[26] As a preacher he assumed a position of leadership in the slave community and acquired a reputation as a seer and visionary who could recall events before his birth and heal diseases by touch.

In his first vision a spirit approached him as he was praying and told him, "Seek ye the kingdom of heaven and all things shall be added unto you" (Foner, p. 2). In one of his later visions he "saw white spirits and black spirits engaged in battle, and the sun was darkened—the thunder rolled in the Heavens, and blood flowed in streams—and

[he] heard a voice saying, 'Such is your luck, such you are called to see, and let it come rough or smooth, you must surely bare it' " (Foner, p. 44). In May of 1828 he "heard a loud noise in the heavens, and the Spirit instantly appeared to [him] and said the Serpent was loosened and Christ had laid down the yoke he had borne for the sins of men, and that [Turner] should take it on and fight against the Serpent, for the time was fast approaching when the first should be last and the last should be first" (Foner, p. 45).

The sign came in February 1831 in the form of an eclipse of the sun. After one delay when Turner fell ill just before the appointed day, the killings began on the night of Monday, August 23 (Foner, p. 3). In Turner's own words as later transcribed by Thomas Gray in Turner's prison cell as he awaited execution:

It was quickly agreed we should commence at home (Mr. J. Travis') on that night, and until we had armed and equipped ourselves, and gathered sufficient force, neither age nor sex was to be spared (which was invariably adhered to). [The seven of them feasted until about two hours after dark; then all except Turner] went to the cider press and drank. . . . On returning to the house, Hark [one of the chief conspirators] went to the door with an axe, for the purpose of breaking it open, as we knew we were strong enough to murder the family, if they were awaked by the noise; but reflecting that it might create an alarm in the neighborhood, we determined to enter the house secretly, and murder them whilst sleeping. Hark got a ladder and set it against the chimney, on which I ascended, and hoisting a window, entered. . . . It was then observed that I must spill the first blood. On which, armed with a hatchet, and accompanied by Will, I entered my master's chamber, it being dark, I could not give a death blow, the hatchet glanced from his head, he sprang from the bed and called his wife, it was his last word, Will laid him dead, with a blow of his axe,

and Mrs. Travis shared the same fate as she lay in bed. The
murder of this family, five in number, was the work of a moment, not one of them awoke; there was a little infant sleeping
in a cradle, that was forgotten, until we had left the house and
gone some distance, when Henry and Will returned and killed
it. [Foner, pp. 45–46]

Salathul Francis's cabin was six hundred yards away
from the Travis place. Two of the slaves knocked at the
door and said they had a letter for him. When he came to
the door, they grabbed him, dragged him a little way from
the door, and killed him "by repeated blows on the head"
(Foner, p. 46). By sunrise, two more homes had been visited
and their occupants killed. From then until nine or ten
o'clock four more homesteads suffered the same fate. But at
one place, the Porters', the family had fled, and Turner
immediately realized that the alarm had now been spread.
He and his band continued on to four more homesteads,
at one of which they killed a Mrs. Waller and her ten children. Turner's band had reached its peak number of fifty
or sixty, and he determined to start for the county seat of
Jerusalem to procure arms and ammunition. Only some of
his men had guns; the others were armed with axes, swords,
and clubs.

At this point Turner and his men were met by eighteen
white men who had been following their bloody trail. The
eighteen were forced to retreat after an exchange of fire,
but they were quickly joined by a small party from Jerusalem on horseback. This combined force routed and dis-
persed most of Turner's band, and he was reduced for a
time to twenty men. This was too small a number to march
on Jerusalem, and Turner had to pause and regroup. By
nightfall Monday he could muster forty men. But during
the night a sentry sounded a false alarm and half his men

fled. Turner scoured the countryside looking for recruits and just before dawn Tuesday reached the house of a Dr. Blunt, which the twenty thought had been abandoned. It was not, and the firing from the house wounded several men. The rest rode on to Captain Harris's house visited the day before. A party of white men was at that house, too, and Turner told Gray that on that discovery "all deserted me but two" (Foner, p. 50). Turner sent the two to rally his men once more, but when no one showed up at the agreed meeting place he "gave up all hope for the present" (Foner, p. 50) and went into hiding. It was ten weeks before he was found, but by that time all the rest had been killed in battle or caught and either hanged or transported (Foner, pp. 45–50). Turner and his men had killed at least fifty-five whites, none in battle, all in Monday's and Tuesday's raids on homesteads. Seventeen slaves were executed; twelve were transported (Foner, p. 5); an unknown number were massacred during the four days just after the revolt (Foner, pp. 11, 19).

In leading his followers on their bloody route Turner saw himself as performing a prophetic mission in accord with the dictates of the Holy Spirit, and as serving as an agent of the apocalypse, which would make the first last and the last first. As a young man he had become convinced he had been "ordained for some great purpose of the Almighty" (Foner, p. 43), and when asked after his capture if he now considered himself mistaken he replied, "Was not Christ crucified. And by signs in the heavens that it would make known to me when I should commence the great work . . . [and] arise and prepare myself, and slay my enemies with their own weapons" (Foner, pp. 44–45). The religious cast of Turner's mind is well delineated by the available evidence. But we know much less of the tactics and ultimate goal of Turner's rising. He was clever and discerning enough to limit the number of his coconspirators and to conceal from them his intentions until the last possible moment. He proved to be persistent, resourceful, and quick-witted in marshaling his forces and then later in eluding capture for ten weeks. Even in surrender he revealed, as Gray was ready to concede, "the decision of his character. . . . When he saw [his captor] Mr. [Benjamin] Phipps present his gun, he said he knew it was impossible for him to escape as the woods were full of men; he therefore thought it was better to surrender, and trust to fortune for his escape" (Foner, p. 51). So we may presume that Turner did have some firm plan in mind.

One element in it was to reach Jerusalem, the county seat, as soon as possible because he had "a great desire to get there to procure arms and ammunition" (Foner, pp. 48–49). We know also that when the conspirators first set out on their work "it was quickly agreed . . . [that] until [they] had armed and equipped [themselves], and gathered sufficient force, neither age nor sex was to be spared, (which was invariably adhered to)" (Foner, p. 45). This statement of Turner's seems to jibe with a remark attributed to him in a letter dated November 1, published in the Richmond *Enquirer* of November 8: "He [Turner] says that indiscriminate massacre was not their intention after they obtained foothold, and was resorted to in the first instance to strike terror and alarm. Women and children would afterwards have been spared, and men too who ceased to resist" (Foner, p. 33). On the basis of this evidence, I think it is justifiable to reject Eric Foner's conclusion about the aims of the conspirator—namely, that the simplest interpretation (Turner was going to rise and murder all the whites) is the best one (Foner, p. 4). But precisely what Turner's scheme really was remains a matter for speculation—a good deal of which must center on the possibility he planned to hole up in the Dismal Swamp and there fend off capture indefinitely.

Two more bits of evidence relevant to Turner's motivation also deserve brief mention. The first is that by Turner's own account (as recorded by Gray) his master, Joseph Travis, was a kind man. Turner says that Travis "placed the greatest confidence in me; in fact, I had no cause to complain of his treatment to me" (Foner, p. 45). Thus Turner's revolt cannot be ascribed to his being the victim of any extraordinary cruelty at the hands of his last owner. The second matter of note is that Turner himself takes responsibility for only one killing, namely, Margaret Whitehead's. In every other case the darkness of the room, the dullness of his sword, or his assuming a station to the rear of the line of march are alleged to have prevented his killing anyone himself. William Styron[27] and others have speculated that Turner's guilt and ambivalence constrained him in his own attempts to kill.

It is implausible that Turner or his cohorts had any firm conception of what effects their rising might have on the government in Richmond. But their actions did in fact precipitate a dramatic and enduring change in government policy. In the fall and winter of 1831, petitions poured into the legislature. Some demanded the deportation of free blacks and new restrictions on slaves. But many other petitioners, fearful of the blacks' rising numbers and of future revolts, called for the gradual emancipation of all slaves and their colonization outside the United States. The governor, John Floyd, was only at the last minute dissuaded from sending a message to the legislature in support of gradual abolition.

During the subsequent debate virtually every antislavery argument later raised by northern abolitionists was heard in the halls of the Virginia legislature. As the Richmond *Whig* commented, "Nat Turner, and the blood of his innocent victims have conquered the silence of fifty years [on the subject of slavery]" (Foner, p. 8). Representatives in favor of emancipation, mostly from the western part of the state, condemned slavery as responsible for the state's economic decline, the emigration of white farmers, and the rise of an idle, luxurious, and arbitrary slave-owning class. Some delegates also warned of the danger of future slave revolts and racial strife. But all favored emancipation only if it was coupled with colonization; many westerners feared the spread of slavery to their area.

Few eastern delegates extolled the virtues of slavery. But the costs of compensation in any scheme advanced could easily be shown to be prohibitive, and expropriation would have violated the right of property. So the move toward emancipation was defeated by a vote of 73 to 58. The legislature then proceeded to pass a series of repressive measures that further depressed the status of blacks in Virginia society, and other southern states followed suit (Foner, p. 9).

But the most enduring legacy of Turner's rising came in the aftermath of the legislative debate as Virginia sentiment, which already had exhibited strong tendencies in this direction, crystallized along proslavery lines. In the legislative debate slavery had been defended in the main as a necessary evil. But Professor Thomas R. Dew of the College of William and Mary a few months later published his widely read *Review of the Debates,* in which he not only convincingly demonstrated the economic infeasibility of emancipation and colonization at state expense, but also argued that a practicable scheme of emancipation would have to permit blacks to remain in Virginia as citizens. His confidence that few abolitionists would find this prospect preferable to the continuation of slavery was well placed. He then went further and advanced a comprehensive and coherent defense of slavery as a positively beneficial institution, basing his argument on historical precedents, scriptural proofs, economic necessity, and racial inferiority. Dew also maintained that the Virginia debate constituted what Uriah Phillips would a few years later term "a blazing indiscretion." It was foolish and reckless to undermine the settled order of society by venting antislavery arguments in public, thereby encouraging future revolts. In later years as Dew's and similar arguments took hold throughout the South, the virtues of slavery were increasingly extolled, and contrary views increasingly subjected to scorn and suppression (Foner, pp. 9–10).

As already noted, it is doubtful if Turner himself gave extensive consideration to the political impact of his actions. Two quite different interpretations of the revolt from a standpoint closer to his might be called the "religious" and the "mundane." On the religious plane the revolt led by Turner may be assimilated to the millennialist ideology expounded by Frederickson and Lasch, who regarded peasant revolts, slave uprisings, and prison riots as rudimentary forms of political action, since "they rest on some sense, however primitive, of collective victimization."

What makes them rudimentary is that they do not aim so much at changing the balance of power as at giving expression on the one hand to apocalyptic visions of retribution, and on the other to an immediate thirst for vengeance directed more at particular individuals than at larger systems of authority. . . . But in neither case does collective action rest on a realistic per-

ception of the institutional structure of a whole and the collective interest of its victims in subverting it.[28]

Whether or not this general description can be fairly extended to the particulars of the August rising in Southampton County, almost certainly Turner's religious beliefs and
sentiments were the decisive factor in his decision to launch
the revolt. Eric Foner comes to the same conclusion in his
analysis. "The Vesey and Gabriel conspiracies [the two
other American slave revolts of a scale comparable to Turner's] drew on political and humanitarian sources as well
as slave religion for their ideological inspiration, while
Turner seems to have been motivated exclusively by his
mystical visions" (Foner, p. 176). Foner also draws an explicit parallel between the slave preacher, Turner, and
"the religious mystics who led the bloody millenarian peasant outbreaks . . . often obsessed for years with apocalyptic
fantasies and visions, who believed themselves chosen by
God to bring about a purging of the world's sins and a new
era of divine rule on earth" (Foner, p. 176). Despite Turner's firm grasp of immediate tactical requirements during
the struggle, Vincent Harding is right that "obviously Nat
Turner was one of those religious charismatics who arise in
a variety of settings, from the walls of Muenster to the fields
of Southampton County." [29]

Since millenarian motives were decisive in determining
Turner's course, there is a sense in which the mundane
level of explanation does not apply to his actions. But when
we do attempt to reconstruct the logic of the rising on this
level it proves to be no easy task, not only because of a pau-
city of information about the slaves' intentions, but also because their actions seem doomed and futile. It is evident
that Turner's plan was to invade the county seat of Jeru-

salem, terrorize its inhabitants, and seize the arms stored there. But what next? William Styron took the view that the insurgents intended then to retreat into the Dismal Swamp nearby and there fend off capture by means of mobile guerrilla tactics. This at first appears to be the most plausible interpretation available, since it seems a relatively modest and attainable goal. But how much can really be made of it? If the number of insurgents never exceeded a few dozen, why should they not have escaped as individuals or in small groups, rather than arousing the wrath of the white community and risking extermination by a mass rising? If instead the expectation was that hundreds or even thousands of slaves would be recruited to the insurgency, the question arises whether the swamp-state could have withstood a concerted attack by large forces from without.

The same objection applies to Turner's plan to establish a "foothold," after which with increased numbers and more arms his forces could afford to spare white women and children. Even assuming that despite the oppressive conditions under which he worked Turner could have done the political work necessary to bring hundreds or thousands to his movement, there remains one insuperable obstacle to any such scheme. Slaves and other blacks were outnumbered, outgunned and outorganized by their white rulers and the rulers' potential allies.

The hopelessness of slave revolt under American conditions is best seen by way of contrast to the situation in other countries where circumstances were much more favorable to revolt. A suitable comparison is with Jamaica, since, as H. Orlando Patterson remarks in his analysis, "The General Causes of Jamaican Slave Revolts," "with the possible exception of Brazil, no other slave society in the New World experienced such continuous and intense

servile revolts as Jamaica." Two stark contrasts between
Jamaican and American conditions stand out. First, in Jamaica the ratio of slaves to masters exceeded ten to one.
Only in South Carolina and Mississippi did slaves even out-
number whites. Second, a larger proportion of American
slaves were born into slavery than in Jamaica, where the
failure of the slave population to replace itself necessitated
continued importation.[30] Those raised to slavery were reg-
ularly less likely to revolt than those kidnapped into it.
Even in Jamaica no slave revolt was of lasting success. How
much steeper were the odds against revolt in the American
South!

The only completely successful slave revolt in the New
World took place in Haiti, where the white community
was sharply divided among loyalists, radical revolutionaries, and bourgeois revolutionaries, and the mother country
was for some time unable to assist the planter class in her
colony. In the United States even white northerners were
in 1831 quite prepared to intervene militarily on behalf of
their southern brethren if any uprising should get out of
hand. At least that is what the reaction of most northern
newspaper editors to Turner's insurrection would lead one
to believe. The editor of the New York *Journal of Commerce,* for instance,

[could not] imagine what infatuation could have seized the
minds of these negroes, that they should even dream of success
in attempting to recover their freedom by violence and bloodshed. Do they not know that in addition to the forces of the
white population among whom they are placed, the whole
strength of the General Government is pledged to put down
such insurrection? that if necessary, a million of men could be
marched, on short notice, from the non-slaveholding States, to
defend their brethren in the South? For, much as we abhor
slavery; much as it is abhorred throughout the Northern and

European States; there is not a man of us who would not run
to the relief of our friends in the South, when surrounded by
the horrors of a servile insurrection.[31]

Any attempt at establishing a slave-run state would have
met overwhelming opposition. But there remains a third
possible strategy explicable at the mundane level that
might have achieved more success. This would be a long-
range scheme to unfurl the banner of revolt as often as
possible, and otherwise to raise the costs of maintaining the
slave system by means of whatever violent measures were at
all possible. As the research of William W. Freehling has
shown, it was a series of slave revolts that slaveholders,
especially in the deep South, most feared. In their view, although no single slave revolt was at all likely to succeed,

a series of unsuccessful conspiracies . . . seemed entirely plausible. . . . Any such series of conspiracies could make [an area
where slaves heavily outnumbered whites such as the Carolina
lowcountry] an unnerving area in which to live. Moreover, a
number of revolts could slowly demoralize a community already plagued by grave misgivings about slavery. Few planters
could continue to salve their consciences with myths about
Sambos if trusted Negroes tried again and again to murder
their masters. . . . A slave revolt had a unique capacity to
sweep away all illusions and to force planters to confront the
ugliness in their system.

Furthermore, congressional debates on the subject could
undermine public confidence on the permanency and morality of slavery. This, in turn, might "cause many planters
to sell their slaves. A wave of slave auctions would produce
'a rapid deterioration of property'; and a sharp drop of
slave prices could bankrupt many planters . . . and . . . lead
to the triumph of the abolitionists."[32]

The potential effectiveness of a series of revolts meant that the slaveholders were well advised to take any sign of insurrection seriously and that *if* Turner's rebelliousness had been widely imitated, it could have loosened the slaves' shackles some years before the Civil War. But the fact is that Turner was not imitated, and the slaveholders of the South proved their capacity to keep revolts well below the danger level. The case for the effectiveness of a series of slave revolts does not prove the effectiveness of one carried out in isolation. With the advantage of hindsight we know that Turner would have been mistaken had he expected epigones in later years. We know also that there were forces afoot in both North and South easily sufficient to lead to civil war even without whatever added impetus widespread slave violence would have provided (assuming that such violence would not have had the effect of uniting North and South in opposition to blacks). It is also apparent that suppression of slave-initiated violence would have been extremely bloody, even if not completely demoralizing.

Much less certain are the probable effects a propensity for conspiratorial and spontaneous violence would have had among the slaves themselves. Perhaps organized resistance of any sort would have been useful preparation for coping with the problems of reconstruction. But it seems more likely that a campaign of violence would have resulted in a severe repression that would have subdued the majority of slaves and forced the violent minority to organize on conspiratorial lines and employ ruthless measures to prevent betrayal by spies or the fainthearted.

Antebellum America witnessed two major slave rebellions other than Turner's: Gabriel Prosser's uprising in the summer of 1800, centered on Richmond, and Denmark

Vesey's Charleston plot of 1822. Of these three Turner's was the most successful; the two others were discovered and suppressed before they fully materialized. In an illuminating essay entitled "Religion, Acculturation, and American Slave Rebellions: Gabriel's Insurrection,"[33] Gerry Mullin attributes Turner's success to his not having assimilated the rationalistic and secular point of view of the dominant (white) culture of his time. "Religion and magic sustained Nat Turner's Rebellion. Executed by comparatively unskilled, immobile, plantation slaves in an economically backward area, this insurrection was neither as politically coherent nor as extensive as Gabriel's. Turner . . . politicized his men by means of dream interpretations and feats of fortune telling and numerology." There was no disjuncture between the grounds of his appeal and the ideological and social development of his followers. But Gabriel, and to a lesser degree Vesey, "based their appeals in political and secular terms," and so,

unlike Nat Turner's magnificent Old Testament visions, which transfigured him and sustained his movement, Gabriel's rebellion, lacking a sacred dimension, was without a Moses, and thus without a following [beyond the acculturated artisans, shopkeepers and free Negroes of the city]. . . . The [Gabriel] conspiracy was comprised of autonomous men confronting religious men. Because of the nature of the leader and the rational, political character of its goals, Gabriel's rebellion never became a viable part of the . . . religious revivals [of the Great Awakening].[34]

The foregoing argument leads to three conclusions. First, it is a formidable task to construct a credible rationale for slave revolt in the American South on the level of the mundane. Taken as a whole, mundane considerations seem to suggest that violence was probably far more conducive to effective repression than to enduring freedom. Second, the great bulk of the slave population was in any event not likely to be responsive to an appeal cast in rational and political terms. Third, the sort of rationale that was likely to be effective and to be credible within the cultural milieu of the slave community was not rationalistic and political but religious and millenarian.

However, this last rationale is not one that we would be likely to accept today as a reasonable justification. It seems to be embedded in a false metaphysics (the apocalypse is at hand) and a vengeful, envy-ridden morality (the last shall be first). Of course, much more can be said about an oppressed people's finding means to express their sense of outrage at the enormous injustice done them and transcending the debilitating effects of despair through the assertion of a new-found sense of dignity and manhood. But it is mere sentimentality to deny the ugly and irrational aspects of servile revolt, at least in circumstances where any reasonable calculation of consequences suggests nothing good can come of the bloodshed.

Consider in barest outline the consequences of Turner's night and day of killing—the lives of some sixty whites snuffed out, the subsequent massacre of hundreds of blacks, the further harshening of the slave code, and the apotheosis of the institution of slavery in the minds of southern whites. The blame for all but the first of these outcomes can scarcely be laid on Turner and his followers. Yet the stark fact remains that this attempt to gain freedom not only failed utterly but had substantial effects contrary to those intended.

25

The Battle at Homestead

No nation has had a more violent labor history than the United States.[35] Undoubtedly, the bloodiest years in all this history of violence were those from 1877 to 1919. The major violent strikes of these years include the 1877 railroad strike, the 1892 strikes at Homestead and at Coeur d'Alène, the 1894 Pullman strike, the Colorado labor war of 1913–14, and the 1919 steel strike. During at least two of these strikes the strikers, and not their opponents, caused a significant number of casualties for which a plausible justification can be advanced. These were the strikes at the Homestead, Pennsylvania steel mill, a part of the Carnegie empire, and the strike in the coal field of southern Colorado. I consider each of these strikes in some detail, first the one at Homestead and then the Colorado strike.

In 1892 Homestead was a town of 11,000 located on the Monongahela River seven miles east of and upriver from Pittsburgh. (The present-day Homestead lies just at the edge of the city of Pittsburgh.) Virtually every man in Homestead worked at the steel mill, which stretched along a mile of waterfront. Boiler plates, beams, girders, armor plate, and some billets (slabs) were manufactured here, where 3800 of Carnegie Steel Company's 13,000 iron and steel workers were employed.[36] Andrew Carnegie owned over half of the company (formed in July 1892), but Henry Clay Frick, its chairman, was the manager directly in charge. Although Carnegie was in Scotland during the strike, it was he who made the decision to break the union.

The union was the Amalgamated Association of Iron and Steel Workers with a national membership of 25,000. In 1892 at Homestead and at other mills, "local lodges were strong enough to determine employment and discharge policies, and even to press grievance cases of little substance." Only 400 of the workers at Homestead belonged to the union, though a last-minute membership drive brought membership up to 750 by June. The union's strength lay with highly skilled workers, and in practice it discriminated against the unskilled, the foreign-born, and blacks.[37] The union was conservative, devoted to maintaining existing large wage differences and, to keep total pay high, it often opposed reductions in the length of the work day and abandonment of the seven-day week.[38]

The 1892 strike came about ostensibly as a result of disagreement over three issues: (1) a reduction in the minimum price of the steel billets by which worker wages were determined, (2) a change in the expiration date of the contract from June 20 to December 31, and (3) a reduction in the tonnage rates at a slabbing mill, a plate mill, and the open-hearth furnaces.[39] The difference over the first issue was easily narrowed to one dollar from the initial three, and could just as easily have been settled. A summer expiration date had been in force for fourteen years. The union regarded a summer date as essential, since the workers could not stay out on strike during the winter for long, but the company wanted its labor contracts to terminate on the same date as did contracts with customers. The company thought that the new tonnage rates were justified by the installation of expensive machinery that had greatly increased output and thus the men's earnings. The union representatives held that the men had suggested many of the improvements, that the new machinery required greater concentration and exertion, and that they were entitled to a share of the benefits of increased productivity, especially since it resulted in technological unemployment.

Although the initial reductions would affect only 280 workers, these reductions averaged at least 18 percent, and it was feared that the new scales would soon be applied in other departments. The workers also feared reductions in the size of the work force.

None of these surface issues was a genuinely significant one. The real issue was drawn in a draft notice sent to Frick from Carnegie three months before the contract was due to expire. It read: "As the vast majority of our employees are Non-Union, the Firm has decided that the minority must give place to the majority. These works therefore, will be necessarily Non-Union after the expiration of the present agreement." The real issue, then, was withdrawal of recognition of the union. "Developments in the industry, the power wielded by the union, and the desire of management to control without qualifications the conditions and terms of employment"[40] had induced Carnegie to set about rendering the union ineffectual.

In line with Carnegie's determination, Frick took an adamant position in negotiations and began construction of a three-mile-long board fence topped by barbed wire to surround the plant. Three-inch holes in the fence were placed at regular intervals. (Frick later told a congressional committee these were for observation purposes.) After negotiations broke down, the company locked out eight hundred men on June 28. To Frick's surprise the next day three thousand workers, both union and nonunion, voted overwhelmingly to strike. The eight union lodges established a forty-member advisory committee, led by Hugh O'Donnell, to conduct the strike. The committee quickly took control of the town of Homestead. "A strict guard was kept day and night around the steel works, and all approaches to both town and mill were watched; no one could enter without the consent of the committee. . . . A system of signaling was arranged . . . so that 1,000 men could be had at any spot within five minutes."[41]

On July 1, J. A. Potter, superintendent of the mill, and several foremen tried to enter the mill but were turned back. The strikers were prepared to take whatever steps were necessary to prevent the entry of strikebreakers.[42] On July 4 Frick made a formal request to the Allegheny County Sheriff, William McCleary, to protect the company and permit free use of its property. The sheriff rejected an offer from the advisory committee to guard the plant with its own men as a device to bar strikebreakers. The sheriff then sent Samuel Cluley and eleven other deputies to Homestead at five o'clock on the afternoon of July 4. No sooner had the deputies stepped off the train at the depot than they were surrounded by a thousand men and informed that no deputy would ever go in the mill alive.[43] The turning back of the deputies was contrary to a vague agreement reached earlier in the day by McCleary and the advisory committee, but when O'Donnell was asked about the agreement, all he could say was "You see it is impossible [to get the deputies into the mill]." The men were perhaps more militant than their leaders, and no deputies entered the plant.[44]

At least a week before the deputies were turned back, Frick had begun preparations to take matters into his own hands. On June 25 he sent a formal request to Robert Pinkerton to dispatch in "absolute secrecy . . . 300 guards for service at our Homestead mills as a measure of precaution against interference with our plan to start operation of the works July 6th, 1892." In response to this request, 316 men were recruited in New York and Chicago. Most were unemployed or drifters, some were criminals on the run, and a few were college boys trying to earn a little money over summer vacation. They were led by a hard core of Pinkerton regulars. They were told that they were to guard the property of a certain corporation, and that the only danger they would face would be a few brickbats thrown at them. They were not told where they were going.[45]

The two groups of recruits were taken by train to Ashtabula, Ohio, on Lake Erie, where they all boarded another train heading south. The last car contained crates of weapons and ammunition, but none of the men were armed, so that the letter of a federal law prohibiting the interstate movement of private armies could be adhered to. The train from Ashtabula stopped at Bellvue northwest of Pittsburgh on the Ohio River, of which the Monongahela is a tributary. There the Pinkertons boarded two large barges equipped with a heavy wooden decking that covered them a few feet above their waterline, to be towed upstream by two tugs to Homestead, which lies southeast of Pittsburgh.

The barges cast off at about midnight and approached the mill before dawn. The strikers had been warned by telegraph from Bellvue and other points along the Pinkertons' route, and many of them already lined the shore above Homestead and fired at the barge in the dark. No one was hit by this wild firing, but some shots did penetrate the pilot house and chimney of the tugs.

As the alarm was spread, thousands of strikers and their sympathizers awoke and ran for the river shore. When the crowd on the bank reached Frick's fence they tore down a section of it and poured through the gap to take possession of the factory. When the first barge came ashore a captain of the Pinkertons on its deck shouted out that they were coming ashore to take over the works and wanted no trou-

ble from the crowd. He then went to the stern and helped
his men throw out a gangplank. It was made clear by
the men massed on shore that the Pinkertons were not
welcome.[46]

Soon after the gangplank was thrown down, two shots
rang out. One struck the Pinkerton captain and he fell
wounded. A mill worker on the bank slumped across the
gangplank, fatally wounded. On the order of the second
in command, a volley came from the Pinkertons' Winches-
ter rifles. Firing was general for about three minutes. During this first exchange, according to an early account,
"J. W. Kline and another detective were mortally wounded." As J. Bernard Hogg, who has written the best history
of the strike, picks up the story, "then a strange thing happened. Guards and strikers alike, both apparently overcome by the audacity of their action, turned and fled, the
workers back through the mill yard and the guards into
the barges."[47] The Pinkertons' recruits, who made up all
but forty of the three hundred men aboard the barges,[48]
had signed on as watchmen, not fighters. They cowered in
the far corners of the barges. In Hogg's judgment, "if the
Pinkerton guards had been endowed with the bravery their
reputation credited to them, they might have taken the
mills without further bloodshed."[49]

It is not known today who fired the first shot. However,
the two least biased witnesses cited by Hogg (a member of
the barge crew and an unidentified citizen of Homestead
who participated in the skirmish) agree that a striker fired
first. On the other hand, three nonstriking residents of
Homestead who witnessed the affair said the men on the
barges fired first.[50]

For more than two hours, all firing ceased. During the
lull the Pinkertons decided not to try again to take the

mill, hoping that the union leaders would persuade their followers to allow them to take it peaceably. The Pinkertons could not retreat because the tug had left them and there was a waterfall downstream, but it was decided to pull out when the tug returned, unless the situation had improved by then.[51] Awaiting the tug, the guards cut holes in the side of their barges to observe and shoot at the strikers in case they attempted a charge. For their part, the strikers soon reorganized and returned to the river bank. They were not fired at. They piled up steel beams into breastworks and scoured the town for guns and ammunition.

About eight o'clock a few of the regular detectives made an attempt to come ashore, or at least announced their intention of doing so. They or their announcement was met with a hail of bullets, and two hours of ragged firing ensued. Sharpshooters on shore began aiming at anyone who exposed himself and angling shots into the parts of the barges where men had taken shelter. Pinkerton sharpshooters were ordered to fire at men with a gun in hand, but anyone who showed himself was in danger.[57] The strikers now ventured to appropriate a local Grand Army of the Republic (GAR) cannon and set it up across the river from the mill. The first shot came in too low; the second was too high. It hit a striker sitting in the mill yard in the head and killed him. The cannon was then brought back to the Homestead side of the river and was placed on the hill overlooking the barges. But the barrel could not be lowered far enough to direct fire at the barges. About noon a former English artilleryman charged the cannon with dynamite and it exploded.[52]

When the cannon failed to dislodge the Pinkertons, dynamite was tried. Strikers tossed sticks of it from behind their steel barricades, but the distance was too great and much of it bounced harmlessly into the river. An explosion did, however, open a hole in the end of one of the barges, giving the striker sharpshooters new targets.

Strikers next tried setting fire to a flat car loaded with oil-soaked barrels and boxes and pushing it down a siding toward the barges. Before nearing the barges it left the track and fell beside it harmlessly. Now the baffled strikers discovered a tank of oil in the mill yard. They pumped it into the river and tried to set it on fire, but the wind and current carried it the wrong way. The battle settled down to desultory rifle fire.[53] One of these desultory shots found its way through a loophole and struck Thomas J. Connors in the right arm as he sat under an open doorway. He died in a few hours from a severed artery.[54]

Inside the barges panic reigned. The regular Pinkertons could not begin to persuade the recruits to fight and could not prevent some of them donning life preservers and jumping into the river. Recruits hid wherever they could: in the aisles farthest from the shore, in the bunks, and under tables and mattresses. In their terror, a white flag of surrender was raised at least twice. Each time it was shot down.[55] As Hogg remarks, "At last the hated Pinkertons were at bay and the wrongs of a quarter of a century were to be avenged."[56]

Late in the afternoon the president and president-elect of the union came to the scene of the battle. The president managed to get some quiet and draw the men around him in the mill yard. He pleaded with them, "If you stop now, if you let these men go, the militia will not come. If you keep on there will be five regiments of troops here tomorrow. Then you will have to surrender and will see the 'black sheep' in before your very eyes. You have conquered;

now show your strength by showing mercy." The president-
elect added, "If you permit these men to depart, you will
show the world that you desire to maintain peace and good
order along with your rights." [57]

Finally, Hugh O'Donnell spoke. Shouting from atop a
pile of beams, he "pleaded for the Pinkertons and asked
that the sheriff be allowed to remove the barges." This
plan was disliked, but a suggestion from the crowd that the
Pinkertons be marched out and turned over to the sheriff
on a charge of murder was accepted. O'Donnell would negotiate with the Pinkertons; the men would allow them
to go unmolested. [58]

The Pinkertons agreed to surrender in return for safe
passage from Homestead and an agreement to ship them
their arms. O'Donnell, sensing trouble, armed a bodyguard
of steelworkers with captured Winchesters. A little after
five o'clock the captives climbed up out of their barges and
began their way up the steep hill above the shore.

By now the town was full; a crowd of all sorts of people
had gathered to watch the battle. Many of them were in a
nasty, vengeful mood; others were mere thieves. As the
guards scrambled up off the bank, they were tripped and
sand was thrown into their eyes. Once they reached the
mill yard, despite the efforts of union men to protect them,
women with umbrellas stabbed at their eyes, stones from
slingshots pelted them, and clubs knocked them to the
ground. [59] A guard who had dropped to his knees in tears
and cried for mercy was knocked sprawling. When he stag-
gered up he was clubbed unconscious. [60] One woman went
from guard to guard wielding a stocking filled with iron.

Once out of the mill yard and into the streets of Homestead, the guards were bombarded with sticks and stones
thrown from the tops of boxcars. Cries of lynching went

up; the guards' clothing was torn from their backs.[61] According to one report, a guard committed suicide in shock after surviving the gauntlet.[62]

Despite this onslaught, the guards reached a place of assembly in town, and, although some strikers were in favor of murdering them all and more wanted to hang a few or hold them for hostages, at midnight all were put on a special five-car train and carried away to Pittsburgh.[63] The battle of Homestead had brought death to some nine strikers and, by one account, to seven Pinkertons, and by another account, to three or four.[64] One of the bloodiest episodes in American labor history was over.

The most immediate and significant effect of this outbreak of violence was to ensure that the governor of Pennsylvania would feel compelled to call out the militia. This he did late on the night of July 10, signing orders that called out the entire militia. Twelve hours later eight thousand National Guardsmen began to march on Homestead. The strikers had no chance against such an overwhelming force, and no resistance was offered it. No sooner had the occupation begun than the company took possession of the mill and began to ship in strikebreakers. The furnaces were relit on July 15, but no steel could be produced without skilled workers, and it was months before production rose to significant levels.

On July 23 Alexander Berkman made his attempt on Frick's life. The advisory committee published a resolution condemning the assassination attempt and extending sympathy to Frick. The outcome of the strike was not discernibly altered by Berkman's act or the response to it.

By November the strike had come to an end, and the union had been rendered powerless. Three factors contributed to this outcome. The first and most fundamental was the economic power of the corporation. The sympathy strikes at other mills were easily beaten back. Improved technology was making the company less dependent on skilled labor. A large number of southern blacks and immigrants needed work desperately and could be counted on to serve as scabs. For these reasons one historian of the strike concludes that "in time, perhaps a year, even without the aid of troops, the Carnegie company probably would have won." Even so, the company was greatly aided in the struggle by the power of the state. Most important perhaps was the introduction of the National Guard. "The decisive effect of militiamen cannot be overemphasized; one searches United States labor history in vain for a single case where the introduction of troops operated to the strikers' advantage. In virtually all conflicts before and after 1892 the state guard acted, in effect, as a strikebreaking agency by validating the right (which most organized workers deny to be a right) of employers to replace old men with new during a strike." [65]

A second way in which the state aided management was by depleting labor's resources as union leaders were obliged to respond to various forms of judicial harassment. This process began on July 18, when O'Donnell and six others were charged with murder during the events of July 6. All but one of them were released after a night in jail on $10,000 bail. When countercharges were brought against Robert and William Pinkerton, Frick, and five other company officials, they were all released on bail before a court hearing and spared the indignity of a night in jail.[66]

On August 30, forty workmen were charged with conspiracy and riot, and on September 22 a grand jury issued 167 true bills against strikers who had participated in the battle. "The indictments ranged from murder to con-

spiracy to aggravated riot. Total bail exceeded half a million dollars [and caused] about a hundred of the indicted
men to skip town." O'Donnell and three others faced with
murder charges were imprisoned without bail for seven
months.[67]

The most blatant and serious distortion of the judicial
process occurred in early October when the Chief Justice
of Pennsylvania, Edward Payson, ordered that twenty-
seven members of the Advisory Committee be arrested for
treason against the state of Pennsylvania. Payson further
decreed that he himself would instruct the grand jury
(which he later did in a way any good prosecutor might
have envied), hear pleas for bail, and conduct the trial if
one were held.[68] There was a nationwide reaction against
this exercise in judicial tyranny, and in time the treason
charges were dropped.[69]

Against this array of state and economic power the striking men and the union stood little chance. In November
the strike was over, but only 40 percent of the original
workers took back their jobs. The rest had drifted away or
were blacklisted. By 1894 the membership of the Amalgamated Union was halved, and it was defunct as a force
within the Carnegie empire. Membership in the union
was reason for being fired on the spot; the adamant anti-
union policy later to be followed by the successor to the
Carnegie company, United States Steel, was already well
established.[70] In only a few years, the union was broken not
only in Carnegie plants, but throughout the steel industry.[71] Not until the 1930s would there be any effective
check on the power of autocratic management in this major industry.

Soon after the strike at Homestead the twelve-hour day
was restored, grievance committees were abolished, wage

scales became a trade secret, and an elaborate system of espionage was established to suppress any effort to organize a new union (Wolff, p. 232). Wages were cut mercilessly; by 1907 those of common laborers in the steel industry were about half of those of the unionized workers in the nearby bituminous coal mines of western Pennsylvania (Wolff, p. 235).

Of course low wages for the worker meant lower costs for the company. "The slashing of wages, in conjunction with new labor-saving machinery, enabled the firm to roll steel rails in 1897 at the all-time-low cost of twelve dollars per ton" (Wolff, p. 240). In 1899 Carnegie wrote a friend, "Ashamed to tell you profits these days. Prodigious!" The firm's historian, James H. Bridge, observed, "It is believed by the Carnegie officials, and with some show of reason, that this magnificent record was to a great extent made possible by the company's victory at Homestead" (Wolff, p. 240).

The cost not counted in this reckoning could be seen only in spirits broken and lives stripped of dignity and hope. After the strike working and living conditions in Homestead deteriorated to depths not left behind until the boom years of World War I.

A miasma of apathy, sullen indifference, and broken spirit permeated the atmosphere at work and at home. Now nothing mattered but a simple matter of survival, of retaining one's job and a bearable standard of living for one's family. Carefully hoarded savings were gone, along with the American dream. Men like Joe Reed, one of the strike leaders, swore that they would never again join a union. Passively they submitted to any terms of work and employer control. It was every man for himself. Cowed and docile, they learned to live with the stretch-out, the speed-up, espionage, the blacklist, the ever-present threat of discharge without stated cause, the en-

larged workday and the diminished paycheck. The only hope
of the more intelligent employees was promotion to better
jobs; and indeed over the years many of them—through dili-
gence, efficiency, and the ability to keep quiet and stay out of
trouble—moved upward on the job ladder. [Wolff, p. 236]

The Colorado Coal War

In the years before World War I, the Colorado Fuel and
Iron Company (CF&I), a part of John D. Rockefeller's
industrial empire, had imposed on its workers and their
families in southern Colorado a regime despotic but not
enlightened. Most of these workers had come to the mines
ten years earlier, in 1903, as strikebreakers. Many had
come involuntarily, kept in their coaches by guards at
either entrance.[72] Their reluctance was well founded. The
firm owned the land under the workers' houses, which
were nothing more than shacks and hovels. Company stores
earned 20 percent per year on their capital by charging
exorbitant prices. Company officials controlled the selection
and dismissal of school teachers and even fired minis-
ters who exhibited socialistic tendencies. The firm cen-
sored movies, books, and magazines, banning the writings
of Darwin and Omar Khayyam. The dominant role of the
company in state politics depended partly on its voting all
its employees (regardless of citizenship). Outright fraud
was resorted to in the casting and counting of ballots, and
the election of judges and sheriffs was rigged by the company.[73]

Under political conditions such as these, the company
had nothing to fear from state inspectors, even though
Colorado mines had a death rate twice as high as any other
state in the union. In ninety accident cases over ten years,

coroner's juries in Huerfano County blamed the operators only once. The truth was that southern Colorado was not governed from the capital in Denver, but by company managers on the spot and in New York. The company felt free to refuse the state superintendent of public instruction entry into "its" schools and had no compunctions about denying union organizers and workers the rights of free speech and assembly. Meetings concerning welfare, wages, and law enforcement were simply not permitted.[74] The violence with which we are concerned here did not erupt within a well-ordered democratic state, but rather under the aegis of a highly despotic regime that denied its subjects fundamental rights and made a travesty of the law as promulgated by the nominal authorities in Denver.

Despite the denial of free speech, so harsh were conditions for the miners that in 1913 the strikebreakers of ten years earlier themselves could stand no more. They struck for an eight-hour day, enforcement of safety regulations, abolition of company scrip, the right of workers to trade at stores of their own choosing, and other elementary requirements of decency. Not surprisingly, most of these demands were for actions by the company that, according to state laws, it should already have been taking. In part what the strikers were seeking was that the company be brought under the jurisdiction of the elected government in Denver and cease being permitted to function as a (despotic) state within a state.[75]

The company could have avoided or at least forestalled the strike by even one noncommittal meeting with the United Mine Workers but chose instead to deny the union any excuse to boast of recognition. In September of 1913 the strike began. As many as ten thousand workers packed their household goods onto carts and, in the midst of a driving snowstorm, began the trek to establish tent cities up nearby canyons. Employees on strike could not remain in company houses on company property.

Violence was intermittent from the outset of the strike as the company immediately hired large numbers of guards and entrenched its men, armed with machine guns, at the edge of its property and provided them with a special armored automobile christened the "Death Special." Both sides were responsible for a number of assaults and murders, and the governor soon called out the National Guard.

The militia at first played an impartial role and went so far as to forbid the importation of strikebreakers. But in less than a month the Guardsmen were being used to escort strikebreakers. L. M. Bowers, superintendent of CF&I, explained this shift in policy in a report to Rockefeller:

You will be interested to know that we have been able to secure the cooperation of all the bankers of the city [of Denver] who have had three or four interviews with our little cowboy Governor, agreeing to back the state and lend it all the funds necessary so that our miners could return to work, or give protection to those men who are anxious to come up here from Texas, New Mexico and Kansas. . . . Besides, the bankers, the Chamber of Commerce, the Real Estate Exchange, together with a great many of the best business men, have been urging the Governor to take steps to drive these vicious agitators out of the State.[76]

At a later stage in the strike, Rockefeller helped to ghostwrite a letter from the governor to President Wilson.[77] As Bowers's report suggests, the state government was not able to finance an extended Guard call-out. With the legislature out of session, it was CF&I that paid and quartered the troops.[78] Later on in the strike, guns were given to mine guards by members of the militia and company guards were inducted into the militia and paid by both the state and the company. The CF&I imported guns and strike-breakers contrary to state law and gave some of the guns to militiamen.[79] By the time violence reached a peak in April 1914, the Guard was composed in large part of mine guards, professional soldiers, and adventurers of various stripes.[80] Not surprisingly, militiamen were responsible for a number of unseemly acts of the sort members of a poorly disciplined army of occupation are often responsible for. And more significantly, by April the Guard had lost every shred of its reputation for just dealing. As an official investigation by George West later concluded, it "no longer offered even a pretense of fairness or impartiality, and its units had degenerated into a force of professional gunmen and adventurers who were economically dependent on and subservient to the will of the coal operators." The state, in the person of the Guardsmen, was without authority in the whole southern mining region, and had become dependent solely upon sheer power.[81] But the tenuousness of the power of the state became fully apparent only in the aftermath of the events of April 20, 1914, the day of the Ludlow Massacre.

Months of constant conflict and sporadic violence had left both sides edgy and fearful. The militiamen, outnumbered, feared a sudden disastrous onslaught from the strikers, who in their turn were well aware that high officials of the company and the Guard would have liked to see the union colonies dismantled. On the morning of Monday, April 20, Major Patrick C. Hamrock, commander of the militia force in the strike zone, received a note from a woman claiming that her husband was being held in the Ludlow colony against his will. A corporal and two men made inquiries about the man at the colony, and did so in a blustery and presumptuous manner that infuriated the hot-blooded Greeks living there. The Greeks' leader, Louis Tikas, sent word back with the corporal that no such man was enrolled in the colony. Hamrock thereupon telephoned Tikas and asked him to come to a meeting in his own tent. Tikas refused.

At about the time of this telephone call, Hamrock heard from his adjutant, who had the colony under surveillance through his artillery field glasses, of an ominous commotion in the colony. Hamrock ordered twenty cavalry men to the crest of a shallow mesa known as "Water Tank Hill," overlooking the colony from the south, and instructed them to drill conspicuously there. Soon after these orders were given, Tikas phoned back and asked for a meeting at the railroad depot, halfway between the major's tent and his own. Tikas, a man of peaceful inclinations, sounded harassed and unsteady, so the major issued further orders that a machine gun be placed atop Water Tank Hill. Meanwhile Tikas made his men promise to do nothing rash and set out to meet Hamrock. But soon after his departure the strikers spotted the Guardsmen prancing on the crest of Water Tank Hill. They now either broke their promise to Tikas or acted in fear of an imminent attack. Some of them rushed to take positions in a sand cut on the right flank of the twenty men on the hill, and larger numbers ran into a wide east–west arroyo farther to the north of and more sheltered from Water Tank Hill than the colony. Tikas, greatly alarmed, ran from the depot back to the tents, screaming for his men to come back. But he was ignored and soon a burst of rifle fire was directed at the men on Water Tank Hill. Possibly this burst of fire was itself precipitated by an anxious militiaman's own shot, but this seems unlikely since the men on the hill were

pleading with their commander, Lieutenant K. E. Linderfelt, for permission to fire, and he refused for some time.[82]

The ensuing battle lasted all day. One militiaman was fatally wounded early in the fray; five strikers and a young
boy were lost. By late evening the militia controlled the
field. Louis Tikas had stayed behind in the colony to look
after the many women and children who remained there,
pinned down by fire, especially from the militia's machine
gun. Tikas was captured and brought to Lieutenant Linderfelt. Linderfelt smashed Tikas over the head with the
stock of a Springfield rifle with such force the stock snapped
in half, but Tikas remained standing. Linderfelt later
gave as an excuse for his action that Tikas "called me a
name that no man will take."[83] A short time later Tikas
was shot three times in the back and died, along with two
other captured strikers.

As the militiamen charged into the tent colony in the
late evening they became an "uncontrollable, murderous,
pillaging mob."[84] As some of them had planned doing earlier in the afternoon, they set fire to the tents with torches
and spread the fire with coal oil. One by one the tents went
up in flames, even as some of the remaining women and
children fled in the confusion and others huddled, afraid
to move, in the pits dug beneath the tents weeks before for
protection. The Guardsmen also looted what they could
and smashed the rest. In the words of National Guard officers who conducted a subsequent investigation, the militia
"had ceased to be an army and had become a mob." The
troops were obviously determined to wipe out the colony
once and for all.

The next morning the sun shone down on the tent colony become a charred shambles. "Militiamen stalked
through the wreckage surveying results of their work of the

night before, the dark [pits] under the tents now exposed
to their gaze. Then came the discovery which horrified the
entire nation and which threw the strikers into a frenzy of
grief and uncontrollable rage. Huddled together in one of
the larger pits were the lifeless bodies of two young moth-
ers and eleven small children." [85] This was the catastrophe
to be known in history as the Ludlow Massacre.

Union publicists immediately branded the deaths as deliberate murder, and this view was widely shared in the
general public, where sympathy with the strikers was widespread, as was the belief that the deaths had resulted from
an intentional massacre. The truth is more likely that the
militiamen believed that they had cleared the village before they set fire to it. The women in the pit presumably
feared to emerge and thought themselves and their children safe from flame. But the fire exhausted the supply of
oxygen in the pits and caused death by asphyxiation. In
legal terms, the militiamen were more likely guilty of manslaughter than homicide with malice aforethought. The
scene was confused and witnesses on both sides biased and
not always trustworthy. Even a truly impartial inquiry,
rather than the ex parte National Guard investigation that
was actually conducted, would have had a difficult task. But
a reasonable judgment is that the strikers (and the general
public) too hastily concluded that the militiamen were
guilty of deliberate murder and that the militiamen exhibited a reckless disregard for human life as they ran amuck
at the Ludlow tent colony.

Through the accounts of the strikers' response to the
Ludlow Massacre run two conflicting themes. The first em-
phasizes the elements of spontaneity and uncontrollability
in the actions of the strikers. They are pictured as having
"gone mad," as being "bereft of reason," and "driven by a

thirst for revenge." The suggestion is that they were so se-
verely provoked as to lose self-control and to be unable to
respond to the report of the events at Ludlow other than
they did. The second theme concerns the extent to which
union leaders, certainly in the state organization and presumably among the local units that carried out the actual
fighting, "planned the movements of their men, set about
collecting and distributing arms and ammunition, and
openly justified their acts." Planning and deliberation are
the keynotes here. The implication of the first interpretation of the strikers' actions is that they could not have done
other than they did in the teeth of so irresistible a provocation. The responsibility for their actions is not really their
own but rather should be placed on the militiamen, whose
actions triggered an inevitable response. The contrary view
of an observer who stresses the element of planning and deliberation in the strikers' response is that "for the events
that followed the Ludlow battle the responsibility is clear.
It rests squarely on the shoulders of the leaders of the
strikes. They counseled hostilities, recruited men and dis-
tributed arms." [86]

Let me now describe the events that followed the assault
on Ludlow in an attempt to reconcile or decide between
these conflicting interpretations. What the strikers did for
ten days after the deaths at Ludlow was to launch a series
of armed attacks against mines throughout the strike region and as far north as Denver. (Trinidad and Walsenburg, where the strike was centered, are near the New
Mexico border. Denver, of course, is near the center of
Colorado.) The general pattern was for a mine to be attacked by armed men who shot any guards that put up
resistance and for the mine buildings and equipment to
then be burned or blown up.

Certainly these activities did not take place in a vacuum of leadership at the center. The very day of the morning on which the bodies of the victims at Ludlow were discovered, union leaders in Denver began to draft a circular to all Colorado labor organizations entitled "A Call to Rebellion." It read as follows:

Organize the men of your community in companies of volunteers to protect the workers of Colorado against the murder and cremation of men, women and children by armed assassins in the employ of the coal corporations, serving them under the guise of militiamen. . . . The state is furnishing us with no protection and we must protect ourselves. . . . We seek no quarrel with the state and we expect to break no law; we intend to exercise our lawful right as citizens, to defend our homes and our constitutional rights.

Union headquarters in Denver and Trinidad were besieged with volunteers. A thousand or more strikers took up arms and seized control of an area eighteen miles long and five miles wide within which the most important mines were to be found. Bands of strikers moved from mine to mine, killing guards—at least those who resisted—and destroying what they could. The Empire mine near Aguilar was the first target. There "the shaft house and buildings were dynamited and three guards who attempted to defend the property were shot and killed." Seven other mines "were similarly fired upon and burned by the rampaging union bands." [87]

A shaky truce between militia and strikers was soon undermined by an attack on a mine near Canon City during which one man was killed. Two attacks on mines near Louisville and Lafayette soon followed. On Monday, April 27, a battle between hundreds of strikers, guards, and militiamen broke out near Walsenburg. The militia was held off while a mine was attacked and some of its buildings burnt. When the battle was rejoined, a three-inch cannon was used against the strikers to some effect. A medic wearing a red cross was killed by the strikers. One striker was killed accidentally, and two noncombatants lost their lives.

The bloodiest battle of the week came the next Wednesday at the Forbes mine, scene of an attack by the Death Special in October. On that occasion the camp had been swept by machine-gun fire that killed a striker and shot an eighteen-year-old boy nine times through the legs as he lay outside his tent. Every time he tried to pull himself into his tent he was shot at again. To avenge these actions as well as the killings at Ludlow, late on April 29 over a hundred armed strikers set out from Trinidad. In the hills groups of strikers joined them. By five o'clock in the morning some three hundred armed men looked down on the tipple, scales, post office, boiler-house, and other mine buildings strung out the length of a mile on the canyon-bottom below them. It is important in assessing the motives of these attackers (were they vengeful or constructive?) to observe that on April 29 word had spread throughout Colorado that President Wilson had ordered the dispatch of federal troops to the embattled area.

The attackers swept in from the south, opening fire without warning. The initial attack was met by fire from a poorly functioning but still deadly machine gun at the northern end of the camp. (The machine gun later jammed and was abandoned.) Three of the attackers fell dead, although the camp was defended by only eighteen armed men. But the strikers swarmed in, dashing oil on every building and piece of equipment and setting it aflame. Nine of those present in the camp were killed: two as they tried to flee the camp, five trapped in burning buildings, and two in some way not reported. None of these victims at the time they were killed posed any threat to the safety of the attackers. But it would be unfair to the attackers to picture them as consumed by bloodlust. Had they been so, six scabs captured by the strikers would have been hanged as half their captors indeed demanded. Instead, after an hour and a half they were turned loose in the hills. Only a few hours later the first unit of federal troops, 125 men of the Twelfth U.S. Cavalry, arrived at Canon City.[88]

In the words of George West's report, attacks against mines throughout central Colorado taken together constituted "an armed and open rebellion against the authority of the state as represented by the militia. This rebellion [was] perhaps one of the nearest approaches to civil war and revolution ever known in this country in connection with an industrial conflict." This was war in the sense that territory was occupied and controlled by one side or the other, battles for strategic positions were fought, casualty reports were issued, and friendly papers published communiqués and charged that casualties on the other side had been higher than admitted.[89]

The government of Colorado was prostrate. It could secure the obedience of its citizens only at gunpoint. The best evidence of this breakdown of authority is *not* the violent encounters between armed union men and the militia and mine guards, but the tide of public sentiment in favor of the miners, the openness with which the union armed its men and claimed a role in the attacks on the mines, the refusal of local public prosecutors to take notice of the killings by the strikers after Ludlow, the degree to which the rules of warfare were the only criteria for public criticism of acts on either side during the ten days of fighting, and, finally, the remarkable ease with which a relatively few federal soldiers were able to establish peace in the first hours after their arrival.[90]

Although there is little evidence on the precise point available in the historical record, I think it is safe to assume that the strikers who destroyed so many mines were not literally driven to do so by an uncontrollable sense of outrage, as many accounts of the strike seem to suggest. What should be said, and can be with some certainty, is that they felt justified in doing at least some of what they did, as did their leaders in encouraging and supporting them. A distinction marked by J. L. Austin is relevant here. "When we plead . . . provocation, there is genuine uncertainty or ambiguity as to which we mean—is *he* partly responsible, because he roused a violent impulse or passion in me, so that it wasn't truly or merely me acting 'of my own accord' (excuse)? Or is it rather that, he having done me such injury, I was entitled to retaliate (justification)?"[91] A violent impulse or passion, of course, does not always necessarily manifest itself in violent action. It can be checked, restrained, sublimated, turned inward and become a canker of despair, or turned outward and expressed in brutality against one's wife or children or in peaceful political action. The possibilities are manifold. Unquestionably the actions of the Guardsmen roused violent passions in the strikers, and they were to this extent responsible for what transpired next. Legally the strikers who killed guards at the mines they attacked could have claimed their sentences should have been reduced since the actions of others had put them in a frenzied state where they lacked normal self-control. But this is to say that the miners would have implicitly admitted their conduct was in need of an excuse and to that extent unjustified. Surely some of them would have wished to go further and assert full responsibility for their reaction to the Guardsmen's provocative actions. They might have claimed that they were "entitled to retaliate" in the way that they did.

Unfortunately the historical record available is much more detailed and complete about the exact nature of the provocation (the assault on the Ludlow tent colony and its immediate aftermath) than it is about the miners' response (their attacks against CF&I mines over the next ten days). Those who were doing the investigating at the time quite properly thought that the conduct of the Guard and company officials in the course of the strike and at Ludlow on the day of the battle was crucial to the explanation of the outbreak of violence and to the devising of steps to ameliorate the situation. But my present concern is different. It is with these retaliatory actions and their justification.

One important question to which the historical record provides no satisfactory answer is whether the strikers who attacked the mines intended to kill as many guards as they could, or whether the guards were shot to get access to mine property so that it could be destroyed. In other words, were the miners bent on murder? Another question concerns the extent to which the attacks were centrally inspired and directed. Still another concerns the motivation of those who took part in them: how many were personally affected and genuinely enraged by the reports of the events at Ludlow, and how many were governed by more instrumental concerns?

It is sheer speculation on my part, but I should not be surprised if some of the union's leaders were aware of the advantages that might accrue from attacks on the mines. The chief of these was the intervention of federal troops, who adopted a much more neutral stance than that of the National Guard. Had the Ludlow battle not been followed by armed retaliation, there surely would not have been federal troops sent to Colorado. On the other hand, the investigation of the strike by the Commission on Industrial Relations under Frank Walsh, which turned public opinion against Rockefeller and management, very likely would have taken place even if the death of the thirteen in the pit at Ludlow had not been followed by war and rebellion. Walsh's hearings proved the complicity of John D. Rockefeller, Jr. in the atrocities countenanced by local management, besmirched his public reputation, and helped lead to the establishment of a company union that marked a shift from brutal despotism to a more or less benevolent paternalism.

There are four apparent reasons for the strikers' attacks on the mines: (1) to avenge the deaths of Tikas and the others at Ludlow, (2) to oblige President Wilson to send in federal troops, (3) to get the National Guard to pull back and cease its harassment of the strikers, and (4) to compel the company to soften its bargaining position. How persuasive was each of these reasons?

Of the attempt at vengeance it perhaps suffices to note that there was only a minimal chance that any of the guards killed at the mines would be among those responsible for the Ludlow Massacre. Moreover, even if the crudity and pointlessness of a death-for-death view of retaliation are ignored, the evidence that the deaths at Ludlow were the result of negligence rather than deliberate choice must be confronted. Manslaughter and murder are not on all fours with each other.

Few of those who participated in the attacks likely did so with the intention of inducing Wilson to dispatch troops. Possibly some union leaders in Denver had this end in view, assuming they were sufficiently shrewd and fore-

sighted. The attacks on the mines and the warlike circumstances in which they occurred may well have been a
necessary condition to the introduction of federal troops.
However few or many of the union men and their sup-
porters intended to induce Wilson to send in troops, this
was the effect achieved.

In achieving this objective, the strikers indirectly also
achieved the objective of getting the Guard to cease its
harassment. Life became much more tolerable for the strikers once they were free from the harsh and arbitrary regime
of the militia and private guards. It might be supposed that
the guards stationed at the mines were innocent of the oppressive actions taken by the guards in direct contact with
the miners, but it is as plausible to say that they were all
members of a unified and coordinated apparatus of repression within which all those who wielded force played an
essentially similar role.

Although the conditions under which the strike continued were ameliorated by the effect of the attacks against
the mines, the ultimate outcome of the strike was only
marginally affected. Although that outcome was not complete defeat of the union, it was scarcely a victory. The
fundamental result of the strike was nothing more than
the formation of a company union and perhaps a sufficient
softening of the harsh rule of the company that it could in
the years after the strike be considered a benevolent, or at
least a less ruthless, despotism.

As a result of the Industrial Representation Plan and
other measures instituted after the strike, housing, school-
ing, and recreation were improved. Compulsory company
stores were eliminated, and the more blatant forms of interference by the company in state and local politics were
brought to a halt. Worker–manager committees dealt with

working conditions, sanitation, and safety; grievance machinery was established.[92] However,

there were serious shortcomings. The workers, having had no voice in the actual drafting of the plan, were indifferent to it and still regarded the United Mine Workers as their sole protection; wages, for example, followed those in the union fields, except once when they were lower. Workers were afraid to appeal grievances, and felt that there was for them no true representation, since their representatives were fellow workers entirely dependent upon the benevolence and good will of the company. 'It did indeed seem to [two investigators in 1919] that many of the miners' representatives were timid, untrained, and illprepared to present and argue the grievances of the miners, and that their experience as representatives was not developing initiative or leadership in them.' Yet this plan, a form of the company union, was the only fruit won by the coal miners of southern Colorado after their long and bloody struggle.[93]

The material well-being of the workers in the southern Colorado coal fields was improved, but they were essentially no freer or more autonomous than before. And, to return to the important point, whatever gains they did make were not attributable to the attacks on the mines after the deaths at Ludlow. Whatever concessions the company made were attributable only to the pressure of public opinion and to the dictates of federal intervention or the threat of intervention. These political forces acquired the strength they had because of indignation at the lengths to which the company had gone, most notably at Ludlow. The retaliatory violence of the miners was generously, and, all things considered, rightly overlooked by the public. It was not a significant factor in achieving whatever gains the company conceded in the aftermath of the strike.

2
Morality and History

That violence on the part of the oppressed can be justified, if at all, only as an instrument of social change is often taken to be a commonplace. Violence is, after all, by its very nature harmful, destructive, and liable to get out of control. The principle that comes first to mind as essential to a sound morality and the survival of society is abstention from violence. Therefore, a heavy burden must be borne by anyone who wishes to argue that violence can be justified.

However, granted the inherent wrongness of violence itself, surely the only way in which that wrongness can possibly be justified is by some offsetting diminution in the even more wrong conduct of someone else. If I do what is admittedly wrong by its own nature, what can possibly justify that action, if not some corresponding improvement in the conduct of someone else who has been doing even greater wrong? Is not such an improvement the substance of social change? Therefore, is not violence to be justified, if at all, only as an instrument of social change?

These are among the questions raised in this chapter. The argument has four stages. The first and longest considers what the fundamental principles of morality are, or in other words, what standards of judgment we should apply in assessing the rightness and wrongness of human actions. These standards are then applied to the violent actions of the oppressed in each of the four episodes described in chapter 1 with a view to establishing roughly how wrong they were and what was the basis in principle of their wrongness.

In the second stage of the argument an attempt is made to apply these same standards of morality to the conduct of the oppressor to see in what respects and to what degree it was morally wrong.

In the third stage of the argument I try to show that a comparison of the wrongness of the actions of the oppressed and those of the oppressor can only lead to the conclusion that the immorality of the latter greatly exceeded that of the former.

In the fourth stage of the argument, however, I reiterate the point just made that the justification of violence as an instrument of social change must lie in the improved conduct of others in which it results. There follows a brief re-examination of each historical episode that shows that none of them resulted in the requisite improvement in the conduct of the oppressor. The obvious conclusion is drawn that the greater immorality of the oppressor compared with that of the oppressed is beside the point since what is necessary to justify the violence of the oppressed is some lessening in the extent of his immorality. Moreover, since the violence of the oppressed did not in any of the four instances result in the requisite lessening, in no instance was it justifiable as an instrument of social change. The commonplace is thus shown not to hold for the violence of the oppressed in the four cases.

Judgment of the Oppressed

Let me turn now to the first part of my four-stage argument, that concerned with setting out the standards of

judgment we apply in assessing right and wrong in human
action. Here I follow the lead of Geoffrey Warnock in his
useful book, *The Object of Morality*.[1] Among the virtues
that are peculiarly moral in character, Warnock argues,
four are of preeminent importance. They are peculiarly
moral because they exhibit themselves in dispositions
"whose tendency is directly to countervail the limitation of
human sympathies" and to make a person sensitive and responsive to the interests of everyone alike. Unlike such
other important virtues as courage and industry, it is logically impossible that their exercise could, at least in ordinary circumstances, result in harm being done to the
interests of others so as to advance one's own selfish interests. These virtues are important because in their absence
things are likely to go badly in the sense that there may be
"very great difficulty in securing, for all or possibly even
any [people], much that they want, much that it would be
in their interest to have, even much that they need" (Warnock, p. 23).

The four preeminent moral virtues are: (1) "the disposition to abstain from (deliberate, unjustified) maleficence,"
(2) "the disposition towards positive beneficence," (3) "the
disposition not to *discriminate* . . . to the disadvantage of
those outside the limited circle of one's natural concern"
(i.e., to be fair), and (4) a disposition to abstain from deception (Warnock, pp. 80–85).

This list of virtues omits any mention of the concept of
obligation (meaning here the narrow sense of the term re-
ferring to what one is bound to do because of some sort of
undertaking, implicit or explicit, rather than the broader
sense in which anything one ought to do may be referred
to as an obligation). Warnock's reason for this omission is
that the notion of obligation can be assimilated to the prin-

ciple of nondeception. The reason one is bound to keep his obligations is not essentially dissimilar to the reasons he ought not to deceive others. Consider the example of promises. The obligation inherent in a promise does not lie in the expectation of performance it may cause the promisee to have. Sorts of behavior other than promising equally create expectations, and yet they are not obligating. Rather, a promise is a peculiar sort of prediction; it is peculiar in that it needs neither supporting evidence nor any ability on my part to say how I know it is true. A promise from me commits me to a truth about my future actions, and if I do not make the prediction come true I shall have spoken falsely. The fault in not keeping a promise, then, consists in *deceiving* the promisee as to what the future actions of the person who makes the promise shall be. In the case of obligation in general, one gives it to be understood, either by words or by actions, that he will act in a certain way. The fault in not fulfilling the obligation is again that one deceives another. Unless one performs whatever action he has undertaken to perform, the act of incurring the obligation must have been founded upon deceit. "What is at stake, in each case [of obligation], is the preservation of truth" or the principle of non-deception (Warnock, pp. 94–117, quotation p. 117).[2]

The centrality and importance of these four virtues is presumably not a matter of great controversy, though others might wish to redefine them somewhat or to analyze one or more of them with greater particularity. It is worth noting that Warnock's virtues would appear to subsume the obligations and natural duties that John Rawls includes among his principles for individuals.[3] (The duties of upholding justice and of mutual respect are possible exceptions but may perhaps be assimilated to Warnock's princi-

ple of fairness.) It is no more contentious to draw a further
inference that the four virtues will serve well as four fundamental moral principles or standards. Having and dis-
playing a virtue amounts to the same thing as regulating
one's conduct in conformity to a principle. A moral reason
would then be a consideration about a person or a speci-
men of conduct "which tends to establish in the subject
concerned conformity or conflict with a moral principle"
(Warnock, p. 86). Some might wish to add to this list of
virtues or principles, but I assume that it is sufficiently
comprehensive to serve the purpose to which I put it here.

When violence is wrong, it is wrong because it violates
one or more of the foregoing principles. The more serious
the violation, the more wrong it is. Thus the more maleficent, the less beneficent, the more unfair, the more decep-
tive each of the questionable actions taken by the oppressed
in the four historical incidents described in chapter 1 can
be shown to have been, the more reprehensible is each of
those actions. I propose to apply each of the four standards
of judgment to each of the questionable actions in the following section of this chapter.

The first of the four standards of judgment concerns abstinence from maleficence. Maleficence is the intent to
inflict harm or damage on others, out of either callous indifference or a positive taste for hurting others outside the
circle of one's sympathies. The harm done to others may
take "the form of actual injury to them, or of frustration
and obstruction of the satisfaction of their wants, interests,
and needs" (Warnock, p. 80). As Warnock further points
out, the disposition to abstain from maleficence "is not, in a
sense, very much of a virtue," since it is, "one may hope-
fully suppose, just normally to be expected in normal persons, who accordingly come up for commendation on this

account only if their non-maleficence is exceptional in degree, or maintained in the face of exceptional temptation, or provocation, or difficulty." Still, we should obviously find ourselves in "a gangster's world" without this virtue so it is of fundamental importance (Warnock, p. 81).

Alamance. In none of the four incidents described in chapter 1 were the oppressed less bloody-minded or maleficent than were the Regulators in the Battle at Alamance. They took to the field with great reluctance only after years of more restrained forms of struggle, and then only under the impetus of the forceful challenge to their rights represented by the governor's assembled army. Even at the moment before the first shots were fired, some of the Regulators drawn up for battle seem not to have fully comprehended that they were about to kill and be killed. They were not nearly so well prepared for battle as they might have been had they spent the months after the Hillsborough riots drilling and collecting arms. The Regulators were neither eager nor well prepared to do harm to the governor's troops. All of this goes to suggest that the Regulators were, so to speak, only mildly maleficent—willing but not fully prepared to kill, and scarcely eager to do so.

Nat Turner. Turner and his followers stand in sharp contrast to the Regulators. They took a great many more lives, killing helpless infants and children. They were in no immediate danger from those they hacked and cut to death. Turner prepared for his bloody business for some months or years, and apparently did so in the absence of any special provocation. Turner and his followers were not defending their lives; they freely took the lives of those who could do them no immediate harm; the manner in which they killed their victims was bloody and repulsive.

Turner's rebellion was a terrifying display of nearly unbridled bloodletting.

Homestead. Like the Battle of Alamance, the all-day battle at Homestead involved a calculated attack by one group of armed men against another. But some of the workers at Homestead in victory revealed a bloodthirstiness not seen among the defeated Regulators. The battle at Homestead may be said to have had three phases. The first lasted from the opening skirmish at dawn at the wharf to the attempt of the Pinkertons to surrender sometime around noon. The second lasted from then until a surrender was arranged in the late afternoon, and the third phase was the onslaught on the captive Pinkertons as they made their way uphill to the point of assembly near the railroad station.

It is evident that the violence done to the Pinkertons by some strikers and many onlookers in the second and third phases of the battle was gratuitous in the sense that it neither could nor did do anything to help prevent the intromission of strikebreakers, nor did it help the strike succeed in any other way. The sole purpose of the violence in the later phases of the battle was to avenge the lives of comrades lost earlier in the day. The victim might be one who had cowered below deck all day and never fired a shot. But even if a victim had been responsible for the death of a striker, must he too die in retaliation? The only good his death would do would be to satisfy the lust for vengeance felt by some of the strikers and townspeople. But since such raw passions only serve to add to the sum total of human misery, it would be for the best if they did not exist or were not satisfied. No plausible defense of the strikers' and townspeople's violence in the second and third phases of the battle can be put forward.

The first phase is another story. It resembles the Battle of Alamance in that the strikers occupied a position in a defensive posture and were attacked in an act that might be construed as aggression. But the strikers seem to have been better prepared and more eager to attack their adversaries than were the Regulators. From the moment the strike began, they were ready to kill if need be to keep control of the plant at Homestead.

Ludlow. Although the attacks on the mines at Forbes and elsewhere were in response to what was taken to be the deliberate murder of innocent women and children, they nonetheless lack the defensive character of the actions of the Regulators and the strikers at Homestead. The historical record does not make certain whether those who participated in these attacks were primarily interested in the destruction of property and killed guards posted at the mines only to achieve this object, or whether instead they wanted to kill as many men fighting for the corporation as they could, and were glad to find, as at Forbes, guards in an exposed position where they could be cut down or trapped and burned. Apparently some of the attackers were more bloodthirsty than others. If some were more restrained than they might have been, as when they released the six captives, it is still fair to say that the attackers displayed no more regard for the lives of those trapped and killed by heat and asphyxiation than did the militiamen at Ludlow. We know that George West in his sympathetic account of the strike states quite plainly that the party of strikers who attacked the Forbes mine were "bent on revenge for [an] earlier attack [on the tent colony at Forbes] and for the killings at Ludlow."[4]

If vengeance was their motive, then the same strictures as applied to the strikers at Homestead apply to those at

Ludlow, except that in the latter case the provocation was greater and that, as we saw in chapter 1, the attacks on the mines may have been intended to bring about the introduction of federal troops and in any event did have that result. It is possible that the attacks were justifiable actions in the circumstances but that the strikers who undertook them were, as moral agents, blameworthy because of the quality of their motives. They may have undertaken a justifiable action for reasons that made them themselves liable to condemnation.

The violent actions of the oppressed in all four incidents were maleficent. It could not possibly be otherwise, since one cannot do violence without intending to do harm. Of the four cases, Turner's Rebellion was by far the most maleficent, followed in some rough order by the attacks after the Ludlow Massacre, the all-day battle at Homestead, and the two-hour Battle of Alamance.

The standard of *beneficence* applies only incidentally, if at all, to the four incidents. Beneficence is the disposition "to give *help* to others in their activities. . . . There are some persons who have particular claims upon the beneficence of particular other persons. And there are some persons who, though perhaps without any special claims, should be helped because their need of help is exceptionally great, or their ability to help themselves exceptionally restricted."[5] Now help is something people may and often do need after violence has been done to them. In some circumstances this is a need that ought to be met by the very person or persons who did the harm. But the obvious point is that this is a separate matter from the justification of doing the violence in the first place, and one that need not concern us further.

A more important, relevant, and complex standard or

principle is fairness, the disposition not to discriminate against those outside the circle of our natural sympathies. Of course, "actual sympathies and natural ties quite often justify discriminatory treatment," but they often do not, and then the standard will be relevant. Fairness is "an essential corrective to the arbitrariness and inequality and deprivation liable otherwise to result from the haphazard incidence of limited sympathies." It is a virtue whose importance tends "to increase with the increase of scope and occasions for its exercise." Many people have the *power* to harm or hurt so few others that most of these will fall within the circle of their natural concern. So "the virtue of fairness—or, more formally, justice—is a more important virtue in, for instance, political rulers, judicial functionaries, commanders of armies, heads of institutions, and so on, than it is in the case of relatively obscure private persons, whose circumstances may confront them with relatively little occasion to exercise it." [6] Warnock's point here implies that the standard of fairness applies better to the oppressor than to the oppressed. But it still applies to both.

Perhaps the most obvious and important application of the standard of fairness to cases of violence directly raises the question of guilt or innocence. Whether in certain extreme circumstances the taking of innocent lives is justifiable, certainly a strong presumption exists against the propriety of any such action. The basis of this presumption is not the principle of nonmaleficence, which counts against the taking of all lives equally, but rather the principle of fairness, since to strike down an innocent bystander is an arbitrarily discriminatory act.

What are the criteria of guilt or innocence relevant in those cases where the oppressed resort to violence? To this difficult question I can provide no definitive answer. But as

a step in the direction of clarifying the issue, it will be useful to set out a threefold typology of the kinds of roles that
may be occupied by the oppressors against whom the oppressed rise. The first role is that occupied in the historical
cases by, for example, Fanning, Frick, Carnegie, and Rockefeller. All these men occupied roles such that they had the
power to take some actions that would have substantially
alleviated injustice done to the oppressed. In particular,
Rockefeller, Frick, and Carnegie could have moved to recognize or continued to recognize the striking union, and
Fanning could have taken measures to reduce taxes and
fees to rates closer to the requirements of law and fairness.
Conceivably if these men had gone too far in righting the
wrongs for which they were responsible, they would have
been deposed by their peers and replaced by new leaders.
But they showed no inclination to do so, and this point remains a speculative one. The term *policymaker* may be
applied to those in positions of high authority, including
the power to agree to and have implemented those changes
in conditions and circumstances desired by the oppressed
so strongly as to drive them to violence.

Only in the relatively simple society of revolutionary
America did any of the policymakers in the four historical
cases actually take the field to confront the oppressed in
person. In the other cases the policymakers (Frick excepted) occupied a more insulated position. The direct
confrontation took place, as it typically does in modern,
bureaucratized societies, between the oppressed and persons occupying subordinate positions within the organization headed or dominated by the policymakers. Those in
these subordinate positions are normally on the payroll of
the policymaker's organization or some other organization
that is acting in the interests of the policymaker. They are

not empowered to take those actions that would bring about the changes in conditions and circumstances desired by the oppressed. If it is understood clearly that those occupying this position do not necessarily belong to the bureaucratic chain of command of the policymaker's own organization, nor perhaps even to any formal organization, then the term *subordinate* may do to describe this sort of role. The crucial features of this role are that it involves acting in the interests of the policymaker and against the interests of the oppressed and that its occupant is not empowered to bring about the changes desired by the oppressed.

There are two kinds of subordinates. The first is typified by such roles as plant supervisor and clerk of the court. These are subordinates proper. The second is a special kind of subordinate, the kind with whom the oppressed is most likely to come into violent confrontation, and hence the kind that is most likely to be the victim of violence of the oppressed. This sort of subordinate may be called a *forcewielder,* meaning simply those who are armed and prepared in their own persons to exercise deadly force against the oppressed. The Pinkertons, the militiamen, and Governor Tryon's volunteers and mercenaries are all forcewielders. Their role is the same as that of other subordinates except that it involves the direct use of deadly force in the interests of the policymaker.

On the field at Alamance, some of the officers may have been policymakers, and the ordinary soldiers were forcewielders. The guilt of the former was greater than that of the latter inasmuch as only the former were responsible prior to the time of the battle for perpetuating the circumstances and conditions that the Regulators found objectionable. Yet if victory on the battlefield was necessary to

the perpetuation of injustice, then the common soldier became, even though his motivation for joining the ranks
might have been merely a desire to make a little extra
money, as indispensable a protector of injustice as any policymaker. In a court of law where "a guilty mind" is required to justify conviction for a criminal offense, the
common soldier might have had a strong case and the policymaker a weak one. But on the battlefield their respective
states of mind made no difference to the outcome.

The problem is similar to a situation that may arise in
war, where some combatants (say, sixteen-year-old draftees)
may in some evident sense be less guilty than others (say,
ardent Nazi volunteers). In battle even if the reluctant
draftee and the fanatic party member could be distinguished, one would rightly shoot either freely as each represented a good target and a source of danger to one's own
unit. In actual combat the criterion of guilt is simple indeed; if an enemy is trying to kill people on one's own
side, then it is fair for those people to try to kill him. In
combat conditions "subjective" innocence is of no account;
all that matters is "objective" guilt. Later in this chapter I
elaborate further on this problem of the meaning of guilt
and innocence when groups of men turn to violence.

Imagine now that the leaders of the Regulators had foreseen the battle between drawn armies and the infliction of
some nine fatal casualties on the other side as well as nine
on their own. In the light of this knowledge could it not
have been argued that it would be preferable to ambush or
otherwise assassinate a few select members of the courthouse ring? Such a strategy of terror and intimidation
might have ended in discovery and executions. But then
open battle also ended in failure, and there should be
some consideration given to the fairness of victimizing the

beneficiaries and administrators of an unjust and extortionate fiscal system and sparing the lives of hapless hired soldiers.

One reason we bridle at this line of reasoning is that it' suggests shooting down in stealth and by surprise men who do *not* mean to threaten the lives of their opponents, even though they do threaten their means of livelihood. This is in contrast to open combat, where everyone can be said to fire in self-defense. (This statement is qualified by the analysis of the retreat rule in chapter 3.) We should also consider that it is fatuous to imagine those who live in a culture where their sense of justice instructs them to spare the lives of subordinates and seek out those of policymakers instead would for long find it practicable to do so, since as soon as this pattern of behavior became evident the rich and powerful would proceed to surround themselves with hired bodyguards who would have to be attacked to gain access to the policymaker. A reasonable assumption is that before the new occupants of policymaking roles were intimidated and reformed they would be well protected by bands of gunmen and well prepared to make the most of new conditions. As long as powerful men retain their power, they retain the capability to insulate themselves from direct attack by means of the services of forcewielders. It is simply not possible to strike at the policymaker except through his subordinates.

The moral logic of assassination seems nonetheless inescapable. It is true, of course, that the forcewielder puts the oppressed who take up arms and choose not to retreat in a kill-or-be-killed dilemma. But the existence of that dilemma is chargeable to decisions taken by a policymaker who in fact or in effect issues marching orders to the forcewielders. On a fair assessment the responsibility and the guilt, if any, is more nearly his than theirs. Typically, a policy-maker in modern society sees no necessity to dirty his own hands by wielding a weapon himself. He devolves that task on a specialist in violence. But the fact that in an earlier and less specialized era Governor Tryon himself took the field sword in hand is more indicative of the moral reali-ties inherent in such confrontations than was the apparent aloofness of Rockefeller and Carnegie. As a contemporary editorialist rightly remarked of the Homestead case, "If it was right to murder the Pinkertons . . . it was right and logical to try to kill the employer of the Pinkertons."[7] The policymakers responsible for the existence of oppression and for the use of force against the oppressed have by their actions made themselves liable to being killed at the hands of the oppressed no less than have the forcewielders whom they hire. Indeed, it would seem that they are more liable, albeit less accessible, than the forcewielders.

Was the choice of victims in each of the four historical cases a fair one? At both Alamance and Homestead (in the first phase of the battle) the oppressed were trying to kill only men who were trying to kill them. Perhaps they never should have taken up arms at all; perhaps they should have retreated if they knew they could do so safely. But at least they were ensconced in defensive positions and sought out by men prepared to kill them. Their criterion of victimiza-tion was fair in that their potential victims were themselves attempting to victimize them.

Furthermore, in the Homestead case the Pinkertons acted without legal authorization, since Frick's lawyers were unable to get the Pinkertons deputized despite their pleas to Sheriff McCleary. Because the strikers were in se-cure possession of the plant and Frick could not show that it would be an exceptional hardship for him to wait for a court order to regain possession, there is grave doubt that the Pinkertons were legally entitled to attempt storming the plant. Frick appears to have been unnecessarily precipitous in initiating the use of deadly force and to have taken the law into his own hands. The strikers technically had no way of knowing that those barges that had crept up on them in the dead of night did not contain a band of uniformed vandals bent on destroying facilities the strikers were taking great care to preserve from damage.

In southern Colorado there could be no claim that the particular men killed in the attacks on the mines were themselves bent on killing the strikers. The victims of the strikers were armed but had given no specific evidence of hostile intent. It was the victims' job to protect company property, and it would have been a dereliction of duty for them not to do what they reasonably could to hold the mines. The miners may have felt that any forcewielder on company pay was fair game, but this is too sweeping and arbitrary a criterion to be allowed by considerations of fairness. Some of the guards and others who tried to defend the mines may have served innocuous functions in the company's organization. It might be asserted that the use of deadly force in defense of property is illicit, but the significant fact in circumstances such as these is that it was the strikers who first took up their guns and confronted those guarding the property with a choice of retreating or resisting. On the criterion of fairness, the strikers in southern Colorado in their attacks on the company mines do not show up well.

I have thus far avoided all mention of the most difficult case, Turner's rebellion. It is evident that the victims of these attacks were not forcewielders. It also seems rather

harsh to say that they were policymakers, since for them to
have sold their slaves and to have denounced the institution of slavery would have been to give up a way of life into
which they were born and raised never knowing any other,
and in any event they lacked the power to bring general
abolition significantly closer. Turner's victims seem in
some respects to fit best into the category of nonforcewield-
ing subordinates. They did not create the institution of
slavery nor were they empowered to do away with it, but
they did play a vital role in carrying out a policy of oppression. Since they could have set their slaves free and did directly oppress them, they seem also to have some attributes
of the policymaker.

The categories of some use in the other three cases here
waver and shimmer before our eyes and produce only
blurred distinctions at best. In the first three cases we dealt
with what might be classified alternatively as: (a) modifi-
cations in the definition of roles or (b) changes in the policies carried out by the occupants of roles. Local government officials were asked to stop stealing, but not to stop
collecting taxes and fees entirely. Company officials were
asked to give their workers a modicum of autonomy and
thus share some authority, but not to renounce entirely
their control of their firms. In contrast, what was asked of
the slaveholders was to give up entirely the role that was
central to their way of life. For them a role was not to be
modified or a policy changed, but instead a role central to
a way of life was to be abolished. In a society in which
slavery is a central institution, it appears to its members
that a "policy" alternative to slavery is literally incon-
ceivable. The institution is so pervasive and dominating
that it seems not to be a human creation at all, but rather

a part of the natural landscape of social affairs. A policy is evidently a product of human choice. An institution central to a way of life appears in a different light.

Slaveholders were not (except in their role as punishers) forcewielders. They were policymakers in that they could have freed their slaves; they were not in that they had no power to abolish the institution of slavery. They were themselves caught up in the web of a way of life in which slavery was an accepted institution of central importance. Yet from the slave's point of view all white men, or at least all slaveholding white men, were oppressors. (Turner spared one family of poor whites on his route.) Even the slaveholder's eight-year-old daughter could order about a fully grown male slave in as imperious a manner as she could muster. Even the infant was cared for by the slave on command and on threat of punishment for carelessness or other misconduct. And an infant might be an heir, as a wife or a child could also easily be. Every white person of the slaveholding class was an oppressor or a potential oppressor in the simple sense that he or she could give orders that the slave was obliged to obey. But if even infants are to be found not innocent, will not the concept be drained of all its meaning and the protections it implies violated? It would certainly seem so. Again, this matter is discussed further later in this chapter.

Still more important from the slave's point of view was the complete inaccessibility of any policymaker other than the slaveholder himself. Even if the conclusion could somehow be supported that the legislators and governor in Richmond were the policymakers responsible for the continuance of the institution of slavery, that fact would mean nothing to a slave in southern Virginia who experienced the violation of his autonomy and dignity much nearer to home and at the hands of his own slaveholder and the members of the slaveholder's family.

The Pinkerton guard who was recruited in ignorance of his mission had a good excuse for being spared the strikers' wrath, but once he took up a gun he became a source of harm to the strikers just like the more experienced and informed professional detective. As a source of harm he was a fair target. Everyone in a position of authority over the slaves of Southampton County was equally oppressive from the viewpoint of the slave. It is plausible to say that as an oppressor, if not as a source of violent harm, he was a fair target. Whether this is true depends in large part on whether a threat to human values other than life itself, in the sense of sheer physical survival, can possibly justify the taking of a life. I try to show in chapter 4 that it can. If I am correct in this contention, then, since to subject a man to slavery is one of the most outrageous ways of treating him short of taking his life, enslavement itself may justify killing to undo the degradation of that status. And it seems fair that the slaveholder and perhaps others who share his authority should be the victims of that killing.

Running through the foregoing analysis are two distinct senses of "innocent." The first, which might be termed the "courtroom sense," means that not all the elements of guilt are present. The requirement of a guilty mind, of knowing, intentional action, is not fully met; some excuse or justification for the action can be found. For example, if one of the Pinkertons aboard the barges at Homestead could have shown he was ignorant of the mission of the expedition, had been unable to get away when he found out what it was, had pressed inquiries about the deputization of

himself and the other Pinkertons, and had not fired a shot
except in self-defense, that Pinkerton would have been
innocent in the courtroom sense.

The other way we use the word "innocent" is closer to
its root, the Latin *nocere*, meaning to harm. Thus "innocent" etymologically means simply "nonharmful." An innocent person, then, is one who is not dangerous or harmful
to others. A person who is not innocent in this sense, it
should be noted, may be perfectly innocent in the courtroom sense.

It is of the utmost significance that the oppressed and
other private parties are typically deprived of the resources
and information that are essential to a finding of guilt in
the courtroom sense. They cannot ferret out, for instance,
the complexities and vagaries of where responsibility for an
onerous policy lies within the labyrinth of a government
or corporate bureaucracy.[8] A judicious finding of guilt and
determination of an appropriate sentence cannot reasonably be expected of the victims of oppression. They must
perforce work with a concept of innocence in the cruder
sense of "not harmful." In dealing with the issue of the
fairness of the violence of the oppressed, the more relevant
and realistic notion of "innocent" must be "harmless." If
the purpose of the oppressed was to punish, this would not
be so. But since their purpose is to protect themselves from
harm and injustice and to seek to force or induce the creation of new social and political arrangements, they need
determine only that a potential victim is a source of harm
and stands in the way of righting injustice, not whether he
is fully responsible for his actions and deserving of death.
But it is nevertheless not without moral significance that
the victims of violence may very often not deserve to die.
That is one of the costs of the resort to violence that counts

against it. Yet the oppressed are not well placed to form the sorts of judgments that alone would avoid incurring this cost.

The only virtue left unconsidered is that of nondeception, which is here most relevant in the form of adhering to obligations. One becomes obligated by giving it to be understood that one will act in a certain way. This can be done either by words or by actions and with various degrees of explicitness and determinacy. Obligations can also be incurred with various degrees of awareness and forethought. "It is quite easy to commit oneself by one's actions without really foreseeing—very often, no doubt, because one prefers not to foresee—just what obligations one incurs thereby." But even if we have not thought what our intentional conduct is going to convey and yet we could have done so, we may then find that we have incurred obligations that we did not clearly intend to incur or admit to incurring. The principle at stake in all cases, however, is the same—the preservation of truth. "We often so speak or so act that, if we are not to *have* spoken or acted falsely, with mendacity, we *must* act hereafter in some more or less determinate way."[9]

The question to be raised here is whether those violent acts taken by the oppressed in the four historical cases were somehow violative of the particular obligations they may have incurred with respect to those whom they victimized. In the Homestead case, the Pinkertons were private citizens and strangers to the strikers, and it is unlikely that the strikers had any particular obligations to the Pinkertons. In the Turner case, there probably existed some personal obligations on the part of the slaves toward their masters, since some relations that give rise to such obligations are likely to develop when people live in close proximity. The slaveholder was in a position to dispense favors, large and small, to his slaves, as well as to afford them whatever measure of beneficent care was regarded as their just due. In the course of some remarkably evocative remarks on house slaves, Eugene D. Genovese says that "The one point I should insist upon in any analysis of the house slave is ambivalence. It is impossible to think of people, black and white, slave and master, thrown together in the intimacy of the Big House without realizing that they had to emerge loving and hating each other." Genovese then goes on to quote from the diary of a Mississippi woman, Eliza L. Magruder, who inherited the management of a plantation. The relationship she describes with her house slave was frequently punctuated by whippings and other punishments for impudence and obstinacy. Yet on one occasion the house slave, Annica, "greatly pleased Eliza by making her a white bonnet." [10] (Only three days later Annica was punished by confinement to her room all afternoon.) At another time, since Annica could not read or write, Eliza wrote a letter to her mother for her. When Annica fell very ill and was in pain, Eliza sat up with her and took good care of her. It seems evident that an intimate relationship of this sort must have given rise to *some* obligations.

I readily concede that most slaves had a much more distant relationship to their master and his family, that much more was expected of the slave than of the master, and even that nearly any obligation incurred could rather easily be overridden by other considerations in what was essentially an involuntary and unjust relationship. But it should be noted that personal obligations on the part of the slave to his master could and did arise. Even William Young's Gilbert, who was one of Gabriel Prosser's assistants most eager to take revenge on whites, said that his

"Master and Mistress should be put to death, but by men under him (as he could not do it himself) because they raised him." [11]

A more difficult issue is the problem of political obligation. I would here adopt H. L. A. Hart's analysis of political obligation:

When a number of persons conduct any joint enterprise according to rules and thus restrict their liberty, those who have submitted to these restrictions when required have a right to a similar submission from those who have benefited by their submission. . . . The moral obligation to obey the rules in such circumstances is *due to* the cooperating members of the society, and they have the correlative moral right to obedience. In social situations of this sort (of which political society is the most complex example) the obligation to obey the rules is something distinct from whatever other moral reasons there may be for obedience in terms of good consequences (e.g., the prevention of suffering); the obligation is due to the cooperating members of society as such and not because they are human beings on whom it would be wrong to inflict suffering. [12]

Although one basis of political obligation is the restraint exercised by other parties to a cooperative activity and the unfairness of exploiting that restraint by not doing one's own fair share, there are distinct limits to what a governmental edict can obligate us to do even if it is generally obeyed. The problem that particularly concerns me in this essay is the relation between the degree to which a government is just and the rightness of taking life for political reasons. There are essentially two possible kinds of relation. One is that the character of the government is relevant to the rightness of certain maleficent acts only so far as it affects the number of alternatives to violence available—this far and no further. The other possibility is that the character of the government has itself a role in determining the rightness of certain maleficent acts, beyond its role in determining the availability of alternative means of action.

The latter possibility represents the correct view. To see why, we must distinguish three sorts of actions that government can take vis-à-vis the governed. The state can first of all prohibit citizens from murder, fraud, violation of contracts and other actions contrary to the tenets of a sound morality. Any government can properly punish people for such actions as these, provided that it uses procedures reasonably calculated to separate the guilty from the innocent and to set penalties appropriate to the seriousness of the crime. There is another set of actions such that no government can properly prohibit them, or can prohibit them only when it is necessary to do so to secure for the general population a minimal rate of economic growth. These actions are typified by those protected in the First Amendment to the United States Constitution, and are those secured by the first principle of Rawls' contractarian scheme of justice, the principle that ensures to everyone an equal right to the most extensive liberty compatible with a similar liberty for others. Any government, however legitimate, can properly coerce citizens who take actions of the first sort. No government, whether legitimate or not, can compel citizens to give up their right to equal liberty, except when the denial of liberty is necessary to the provision of minimal material needs. In both cases the legitimacy of the government makes no difference as to the propriety of coercion; it is the nature of the actions prohibited that is decisive.

Governments also require certain positive acts from citizens, acts that necessarily signify support of the institutions requiring them. These acts include serving in the armed forces and paying taxes. Whether the performance of these acts is acceptable may depend entirely on whether the government is regarded as legitimate and worthy of support. (In the case of conscription into service in a foreign war not necessary to the security of the country, it may also be relevant to consider the precise purposes for which the war is being fought. A government regarded as legitimate may nonetheless undertake objectionable military adventures abroad. But since one of the duties a soldier undertakes on entering armed service is to obey orders, and since these orders may be to assist in putting down a rebellion, military service is always supportive of the government regardless of its position in foreign lands.) The legitimacy of the government is determinative of the propriety of resistance to its attempts to coerce citizens into paying taxes and serving in the armed forces, rather than into surrendering liberties rightfully theirs or abstaining from wrongs that are improper in the "state of nature."

If a government is illegitimate and unjust, it is fair to conclude that some of its officials may properly be regarded as agents of oppression and may as such be subject to maleficent treatment. These officials would include, for instance, forcewielders assigned the task of suppressing protests against attempts by the government to deny those fundamental rights that everyone retains except in the most extraordinary circumstances, but would not include railway clerks or postmen. The line is hard to draw, but just as it is utter nonsense not to hire communists as sorting clerks in the post office even if they are potential spies, it is utterly unfair to kill any employee of an unjust government regardless of the nature of his duties.

The fundamental point about the rightness of killing and the legitimacy of government is that any government is well justified in making deliberate homicide a crime. Moreover, any government, whether legitimate or not, could conceivably take or permit actions such that homicide might be justified in response to them. Only infrequently would a legitimate government not leave open to aggrieved citizens alternatives short of homicide, but it may on occasion fail to do so. It is hard to see how one's specifically political obligation to abstain from violence (because this restriction on liberty is submitted to by other members of political society) can significantly alter in any way one's natural duty to all human beings alike, regardless of their role in a cooperative enterprise, to abstain from violence. The status of a prohibition against killing as one of the rules of a collective enterprise observed by all alike neither strengthens nor weakens the validity of one's natural duty to forbear to kill. In any circumstances in which resort to homicide was justified by considerations such as self-defense or the prevention of some other outrage against oneself, the existence of an obligation to others in a common cooperative enterprise to forbear could not possibly have decisive weight, since in such circumstances considerations of self-defense would easily outweigh considerations of political obligation. The members of a cooperative enterprise could not reasonably expect any member to surrender so fundamental a right as self-defense. My view here presupposes that there exist certain rights in the strong sense that it would be wrong to interfere with their exercise, "or at least that some special grounds are needed for justifying any interference," and that when a person has such a right the government does wrong to try to stop him exercising it.[13]

The foregoing argument implies that had there existed a well-drawn statute that described the circumstances in

which either the Regulators, Turner's men, or the strikers
at Homestead and Ludlow found themselves and then went
on to state that in just these circumstances, a resort to the
use of deadly force was forbidden, then the existence of
that statute could not have been a decisive consideration
counting against the moral propriety of what they did.
This is true because there exists a natural duty to abstain
from violence of such great force that a statutory enact-
ment cannot add significantly to it, and because the only
considerations that could possibly override this duty would
be of so compelling a nature that no obligation under a
statute could stand against their weight.

The application of the standards of moral judgment
derived from the four virtues in Warnock's account of the
object of morality to the violence of the oppressed in four
historical cases leads then to a number of conclusions about
those respects in which their violence was violative of
moral principles. First, the criterion of benevolence is of
no great relevance in assessing the violence of the oppressed. Second, the criterion of nondeception or adher-
ence to obligations is not very important in assessing their
actions, since the personal relationships between the oppressed and their victims were mostly distant, and political
obligations could not have had much force in the circumstances that obtained in these cases.

The most relevant and important criteria are nonmaleficence and fairness. It is the very nature of violence to be
harmful and to cause damage. Nonmaleficent violence is a
contradiction in terms. But maleficence can vary in degree
and can, as Warnock recognizes, be justified in some circumstances. Of the four historical episodes, Turner's rebellion was much the most maleficent and as such the
presumption against its being justified the strongest. The

extent of the harm intended by the oppressed in the other three episodes was less, in part merely because armed opposition made their task more difficult. The Regulators especially seem to have taken to killing with considerable reluctance, whereas the strikers at Homestead and Ludlow were more eager for battle.

The criterion of fairness I have taken to bear primarily on the incidence of victimization. Were the victims of the violence of the oppressed "guilty"? What meaning should be given this term? At Alamance and Homestead in the early stage of the battle all those victimized by the oppressed were themselves armed and apparently prepared to kill the oppressed. In southern Colorado the men victimized were armed and defending the property of an oppressive policymaker, but they did not endanger the lives of the oppressed before they were attacked. In Southampton County the victims of the oppressed were unarmed and offered no danger to the physical survival of the oppressed, nor were they likely to do so in the future. Yet all those killed were or would soon become administrators of oppression in the sense that they would issue orders that were founded on a specious and illegitimate form of authority inconsistent with the right of all men to be free. They were in this sense sources of harm. But it must be added that if infants could be killed as potential sources of harm, then the idea of noninnocence would have been stretched so wide as to be worthless. Nor can it fairly be said that unarmed women were noninnocent in the undeniable way that the victims of the oppressed at Alamance and Homestead (early in the day) were. When coupled with the difficulty of finding the strategic rationale of Turner's actions, these doubts about the noninnocence of Turner's victims give rise to a strong suspicion that Turner was acting as a vengeful judge and hangman as much or more than he was serving his people in the role of liberator. His reported intention to spare women and children after inspiring sufficient terror to obtain a foothold does not outweigh the enormity of the deeds done in the hope of enabling himself to act with restraint later.

By resorting to violence, the oppressed in the four historical episodes violated some of the fundamental principles of morality. But they were also themselves victims of the violation of these principles by their oppressors. It is the nature and degree of these latter violations that I want to delineate next.

Judgment of the Oppressors

Let us begin again with the principle of nonmaleficence. It is evident that the Regulators were victims of maleficence in that severe economic hardships were imposed on them, or at least that they were subjected to arbitrary seizure of their property that was annoyingly harmful. Their sense of economic security and their ability to make plans for the future were undermined.

The slaves of Southampton County were subjected to harsh and painful physical punishment. Neither their clothing nor their housing was warm enough in winter; only the thickness of a single board kept out the cold, and many slaves went without shoes throughout the winter.[14] Moreover, slaves were denied even that modicum of education that is essential to coping with life free of the trammels of superstition and ignorance. They were denied the prerequisites of a full recognition and development of their human potentialities, their humanity stunted and dwarfed.

Their own inner and cultural resources overcame in remarkable and impressive ways the harsh effects of not being
free to be taught and to learn as they could, but this fact
cannot mitigate the maleficence of the imposition of exter-
nal restrictions on the development of the mind and personality. This horrid abuse of the human spirit is a sort of
murder; it does not stop the functions of the body, but poi-
sons and desiccates all that physical survival makes possible,
that is most promising, lovely, and valuable in mankind,
that is distinctively human, and that discerns and assigns
meaning and creates hope.

To understand this abuse of spirit best, one may ask
with W. E. B. DuBois why slavery was so objectionable if
the living conditions of slaves compared reasonably well
with other laborers not enslaved. His answer was that there
was "a real meaning to slavery different from what we may
apply to the laborer today. It was in part psychological, the
enforced personal feeling of inferiority, the calling of another Master; the standing with hat in hand. It was the
helplessness. It was the defenselessness of family life. It was
the submergence below the arbitrary will of any sort of individual." This latter respect is the most vital in differenti-
ating slavery from other forms of labor and in distinguish-
ing its own essence. Eugene Genovese goes to the heart of
the matter when he cites Hegel, who argued that "slavery
constituted an outrage for, in effect, it has always rested on
the falsehood that one man could become an extension of
another's will. If one man could so transform himself, he
could do it only by an act of that very will supposedly being
surrendered, and he would remain so only while he himself chose to." [15]

The maleficence of the industrial autocrats at Homestead and the eastern slope of Colorado resembles that of

the slaveholder, though it was substantially less virulent and destructive. The preventable industrial accidents that killed and maimed, the debilitating effects of long hours and days of onerous work, the degrading and stultifying effects of the wider social environment, the sense of impotence and heteronomy in which suppression of union resulted—these were all fruits of the irresponsible and unbridled sway of capital. The formal freedom to seek work elsewhere and to negotiate terms of work as an individual was of little worth in reality. The acquisition of skills in short supply could raise an employee's wages, and every employer was obliged to meet some minimum wage rate set in the market. But the fluctuations of the free market could have harsh effects, and corporate oligarchs often had a great deal of control over market conditions and could depress wages on their own initiative. The maleficence of Carnegie, Frick, and Rockefeller was less than that of the southern slaveholder, but was very substantial nonetheless.

To some degree the oppressors in the historical episodes failed also to adhere to the principle of beneficence. This is perhaps least so in the case of the courthouse ring in Orange and nearby counties, but even in this instance the extreme financial distress of some citizens perhaps made charitable assistance by those who could afford it obligatory. Less controvertibly, some slaveholders failed to take the minimum care of their slaves that considerations of beneficence would require. The failure of the employers of the strikers at Homestead and Colorado to provide for payment of disability benefits and sick pay may also be taken as a breach of the principle of beneficence.

More important and more complex is the application of the standard of fairness to the actions of the oppressors in the historical episodes. Stealing is maleficent but also unfair, since it involves a transferal of property by taking advantage of superior power in disregard of legitimately based claims of entitlement. The levying of "taxes" and "fees" under color of public authority for purposes of private gain is tantamount to theft and should be regarded as such. This sort of activity is gravely unjust as well as maleficent.

Slavery in America was unjust in that it was based on racial discrimination; to be made a slave because of the color of one's skin (and his birthplace) is grossly unfair. Beyond this it is unjust to deprive anyone of equal liberty without conforming to the requirement of due process that the deprivation of liberty be shown to be necessary to the preservation of the fundamental rights of others, as when criminals are punished, or shown to be necessary to the establishment of a system of ordered liberty such that the liberty of all alike is maximized, as when certain restrictions on economic activity are imposed. Manifestly to deprive a person of all his fundamental liberties solely on the criterion of accidents of birth is as unfair an action as can be imagined.

The issues raised by application of the criterion of fairness to a failure to extend recognition to a labor union are more complex than those connected with slavery and theft. What is at stake in a strike for recognition is power and the question of whether it should be shared. If management recognizes and bargains with an independent labor union, it must then share some of its control or influence over the setting of wages and the determination of working conditions with its employees acting through the agency of their union. If there is no union that needs to be dealt with, then the employer can unilaterally and freely set any terms of work that market conditions and his own market power permit him to set.

One can conceive of radically different ways of organizing economic enterprises such that a division of authority between employer and employee would not exist. But short of the very abolition of these roles, there are strong reasons why the laws and mores of a people should be conducive to the formation of labor unions and should require their recognition by employers. The dignity and the autonomy of the worker will be diminished if he has no influence or control over the terms on which he works. In recognizing a union and sharing his power over terms of work, an employer also enhances the dignity and autonomy of his employes.

The argument for unionization in some ways resembles the argument for political democracy, though it may also imply that unionization ought properly to be taken only as a station on the way to the ideal of workers' control. The premise of political democracy is the idea of political equality, that all citizens alike are entitled to an equal say in the determination of a constitution and of policy under that constitution. An unprejudiced examination of the functions of the corporation in modern society will reveal that in its shaping of the environment in which the worker spends much of his time and in its determination of the economic and status role the employee will occupy in society at large, the corporation is as important as government in affecting the most basic interests, needs, and wants of the worker. Since it plays so important a role and since governments often grant the corporation much autonomy, the idea of political equality should be taken to require that the worker have some considerable say in determining the constitution and policies of the corporation for which he works. The existence of the union that bargains over wages and working conditions rather narrowly construed is a modest and inadequate but nonetheless vital step in the direction of checking the autocracy of the employer and democratizing his rule. If fairness in the political arena requires the right to vote, fairness in the marketplace requires recognition of labor unions. Otherwise power is unduly concentrated, and those who should share it are illegitimately discriminated against.

Since the oppressors were in positions of power, they were more likely than the oppressed to have incurred obligations they might fail to fulfill. A look at the four episodes confirms that what was probable did indeed occur. The local government officials in the Piedmont counties of North Carolina, for instance, had taken oaths of office and knowingly assumed specific responsibilities that were inconsistent with their extortionate activities. They were pledged to conduct their offices lawfully and in the public interest, and were therefore guilty of a form of deception by violating the obligations they were pledged to carry out.

It might be argued that the criterion of obligation is the one score on which the slaveholder comes off lightly in this assessment of the wrongdoing of the oppressor. So minimal, it might be said, were the expectations of the role of slaveholder that in assuming it they undertook to do little for the slave. No doubt in some instances even these minimal obligations—not to starve the old, not to punish sadistically—were violated, since there were few effective legal or even social sanctions on the behavior of the slaveholder. But the main point would be that undertaking to be a slavemaster rather resembles a promise to do an evil thing in that it should not be carried out and, all things considered, is without controlling force.

There is some truth in this view. Southern slavery was a paternalistic institution, and, as Eugene D. Genovese points out, "Southern paternalism, like every other paternalism, had little to do with Ole Massa's ostensible benevolence, kindness, and good cheer. It grew out of necessity to discipline and morally justify a system of exploitation. It did encourage kindness and affection, but it simultaneously encouraged cruelty and hatred." Nevertheless, "paternalism's insistence upon mutual obligations—duties, responsibilities, and ultimately even rights—implicitly recognized the slave's humanity." It recognized "not only their free will but the very talent and ability without which their acceptance of a doctrine of reciprocal obligations would have made no sense."[16]

Within the unjust institution of slavery there existed limits and requirements imposed on the master as well as the slave. However inadequate, obligations did exist, and they were by no means always taken lightly (Genovese, pp. 67–68, 75–86, 123–33). Many slaveholders felt a strong sense of numerous specific obligations to their slaves. In the words of one of them, "to graduate [the slave's] labors to his capacities . . . [to bestow] upon him a fair proportion of the fruits of his industry . . . to improve his mind in correspondence with his condition . . . [to teach] him his moral duties . . . to punish only in compliance with his deserts, and never in brutality or wantonness" (Genovese, p. 77). So strong was this sense that Genovese concludes that "the recurrent themes of duty and burden . . . however self-serving and self-deceiving, constituted the rock on which the slaveholder's ideology, morality, and self-image had had to be built" (Genovese, p. 85).

Significant obligations, then, did bind the southern slaveholder. But it was in the nature of slavery that these obligations were bound to be violated. Indeed, the status of being a slave is logically at odds with the status of being one to whom obligations are owed. It was logic and not perversity that drove one of the finest of southern jurists to rule "that slavery, by definition, made the slave into an extension of the master's will." As Genovese says (pp. 35, 37), once this necessary absurdity was enunciated, "cruelty could only be recognized in its more extreme manifestations; cruelty, that is, could not easily be defined in a master-slave relationship." Nor indeed could any obligation owed the slave by the master. The central ideological tenet of mutual obligations and the necessary legal fiction that the slave had no will of his own could not be reconciled. But the fiction guaranteed that under slavery, as Mary Boykin Chesnut, the most clear-sighted and humane of her class, noted, "men and women are punished when their masters and mistresses are brutes, not when they do wrong" (Genovese, p. 67). As the descendant of one master saw it, the subordination of the slave gave rise in his master to "an unconquerable pride . . . the pride of unchallenged domination, of irresponsible control of others" (Genovese, p. 94). Paternalistic slavery required the slaveholder to believe in his obligations to the slave and to crush in the slave any signs of the independent spirit that entitled any man to decent treatment. One planter, Genovese reports, "said that masters were generally kind but added, 'Against insubordination alone, we are severe.' " (Genovese, p. 87). That is, only against the display of an independent judgment and will—only the mark of humanity. Slavery and the sense of obligation were not genuinely compatible. As one planter wrote in his will, "there is no such thing as having an obedient and useful slave without painful exercise of undue and tyrannical authority" (Genovese, p. 87).

About the wrongness of slavery, there exists today a social consensus embedded in the law. There exists a weaker consensus that the employer is in certain circumstances obligated to recognize and bargain with a union. The norm that workers are entitled to some share of the revenue of an enterprise greater than a minimum wage can be appealed to effectively in many instances. In some regions of the country and some sectors of the economy these notions are less adhered to than in others. But probably all workers, even those effectively denied the right to join a union, benefit from its general acceptance on the commanding heights of the economy. At any rate, certainly today every employer has an obligation to recognize and bargain with a union in a more or less wide set of circumstances, and he is also obligated to let his workers have a fair share of the revenues of the firm in increased wages. These assertions can plausibly be made of all employers nowadays. They could also have been applied, much more controversially, to Carnegie in 1892 and to Rockefeller in 1914. Indeed, the latter man seems himself to have felt their force and to have acknowledged it in an inadequate way by formation of a company union.

Less was expected of employers in 1892 and 1914 than today. But it still would have been enlightened and sensible to say then, as now, that in their position of power and privilege they were obligated to share some modicum of their revenues and their power with the employees whom they had hitherto hired and fired at will and paid as they saw fit. It would have been right to say that one of their responsibilities was to ensure the welfare of their workers, and that another was not to strip them of their sense of dignity and autonomy by standing over them as an economic autocrat.

The oppressor is one who is possessed of great power

and uses it hurtfully and unfairly. To show that those against whom the oppressed in the four historical cases rebelled violated the standards of conduct implied by the moral virtues is merely to show that they were indeed oppressors. Warnock remarks of the virtue of fairness that it is peculiarly applicable to those with power and responsibilities extending to large numbers of people. Hence the potentiality for massive injustice inheres in the role of oppressor more than the role of the oppressed, merely because the former is powerful and the latter is weak, at least until the latter may succeed in reversing their roles. The power of the oppressor also enables him to be more systematically and extensively maleficent than the oppressed ordinarily can. And along with power one naturally tends to acquire extensive obligations as well. Thus it is not at all surprising to find that in the four historical episodes the immorality of the oppressor was in each instance more enduring, general, and grievous than that of the oppressed.

This was especially true on the important criteria of fairness and nonmaleficence, clearly in the case of fairness and less so in the case of nonmaleficence. As for fairness, we must consider either of two sorts of unfair actions taken by the oppressor: (1) violence directed against the oppressed in the course of the conflict and (2) those oppressive actions that did not inherently involve violence and yet drove the oppressed to resistance and violence. We have also to consider the violence of the oppressed and its fairness. The controlling question about the fairness of the incidence of violence I take to be one that its victims can ask, namely, "Why me?" That is, "What had I, apart from all others, done that made me deserve to be the object of your maleficent actions?" I want to compare the convincingness of the answer that the victim of the oppressed and of the oppressor might give and to argue that generally the unfairness of the violence or oppression of the oppressor is greater than that of the oppressed.

Comparison and Conclusion

To begin with the case of the Regulators, if the local government official were asked by the victim of his extortion, "Why me?" the official's answer, if it were honest, would be that his victim is weak and the official has great power and a strong desire for more money. Not much of an answer at all. If one of the armed men in the ranks of the Regulators drawn up at Alamance could have asked "Why me?" of one of the men arrayed against him, the answer would have been "To ensure that you go on having your money unfairly taken as in the past." And the same assessment of the import of what his opponent was doing would serve as the Regulator's answer to the question "Why me?" put to him by one of his opponents. There was nothing fair in the incidence of extortion, nor could there be. The violence of the governor and his troops served to perpetuate an extortionate regime, and the violence of the Regulators was directed against those who were using force to that end. In respect to fairness the Regulators had a much stronger case than did the soldiers who opposed them in battle or the officials who stole from them in peace.

The slaves of Southampton County had no call to ask why they were being singled out to be murdered in their beds. But they could well have asked why they should have been singled out to be made a slave, and there could, of course, have been no semblance of a valid argument that this had been fairly done. But the slave asked by his victim

"Why me?" could have answered, "Because you are my oppressor (or potential oppressor)."

At Homestead the Pinkerton who made that query could have been told it was because he was attacking the strikers without legal authorization in an effort to compel them either to work on terms dictated by Frick or to surrender their jobs to strikebreakers imported from outside the community. Whatever the Pinkertons' subjective intentions ("I'm just following orders, earning a day's pay"), his task was in actuality to compel the workers to give up their union so that their employers could make more money.

In southern Colorado it is quite true that the "Why me?" of the guards at the mines attacked might well have had a ring of genuine and justified indignation. But this was no more than the similar query of many victims of violence by company-hired guards and militiamen in the earlier days of the strike and much less than the women and children in the pits at Ludlow, even granted that they were the victims of culpable negligence and not deliberate murder. Moreover, underlying the whole attempt to struggle against the power of the company was the appalling unfairness of the harsh treatment to which the strikers had been subjected over the years before the strike began.

In respect to maleficence, at Alamance the financial distress and ruin of many farmers must be weighed against the only moderately severe casualties inflicted on soldiers who knew what they were getting into if not what they were fighting for. In Turner's case, an extreme form of human degradation must be weighed against the terrifying slaughter of dozens of unsuspecting persons asleep in their beds or going innocently about their daily business.

The morning phase of the battle at Homestead sets one or two fatalities among the Pinkertons[17] against a like num-

ber of deaths among the strikers and the maleficence of the
lives of degradation that the company sought to impose on
their workers by taking over the plant, permitting the entry of strikebreakers, and breaking the power of the union.
Similarly, in southern Colorado the continued degradation
of life without the protection of union, as well as the scale
of the violence initiated by the company, must be set
against the rather less effective (and usually defensive or
retaliatory) violence of the union and its men.

Thus both a conceptual analysis of the notion of oppression and an empirical comparison of the violence of the
oppressed with the actions of the oppressor lend support
to the conclusion that the immorality of the oppressor is
greater than that of the oppressed, even when they resort
to violence. But this conclusion, however well substanti-
ated, cannot possibly justify the resort to violence by the
oppressed as long as violence is regarded as an instrument
of social change. For violence as an instrument of social
change to be justified it is necessary that the diminution in
the immoral conduct of the oppressor be sufficient to offset
the wrongness of the violations of moral principles by the
oppressed. If no diminution results, or if the conduct of the
oppressor becomes increasingly immoral, then the immorality of the oppressed will not have brought about the
social change that was to have served as its justification.
The oppressed will have violated moral principles, will
have acted unfairly or at least maleficently. The wrongness
of their actions will stand. If the justification of their actions was to have been an offsetting improvement in the
conduct of the oppressor, and that improvement does not
come about, then the actions of the oppressed must stand
condemned.

Notice that the distribution of responsibility in a defense

of the violence of the oppressed is based on the achievement of social change. When the oppressed resort to violence to make the oppressor behave less immorally (perhaps
indirectly by inducing third parties to use their influence
to change his behavior), they thereby assume responsibility
for changing the conduct of the oppressor. Yet the oppressor may well retain, despite his opponents' best efforts, the
freedom and inclination to continue exercising his responsibilities as he sees fit. The substance of social change
is better conduct on the part of the oppressor, or, what may
come to the same thing, a reduction in his power. If the
justificatory ground of a resort to violence is the achievement of social change, then no credit can be given for mis-
guided attempts to bring about change. Failure will mean
that the oppressed are left with the full responsibility for
the harm that they have chosen to inflict and that they cannot point to any offsetting diminution in the immorality
of what the oppressor is doing on his responsibility. Anyone who does violence for purposes of reforming another
person's conduct thereby becomes his (evil) brother's keeper. If that brother successfully resists attempts at coercion,
his keeper is left in the lurch, responsible for the harm that
he has done and unable to point to any compensatory improvement in the conduct of his brother.

The test of the rightness of violence as an instrument of
social change is not, then, a comparison of the wrongness
of the violation of principle by the oppressed with the
wrongness of the violation of principle by oppressor. The
test instead is the question whether the decrement in violations by the oppressor is greater than the wrongness of the
violations by the oppressed. Is the diminution in the immorality of the oppressor sufficient to offset the immorality
of the violence of the oppressed?

There is little difficulty in answering this question in the four historical episodes recounted here. The outcome of the Battle of Alamance was the reassertion of government control and a consequent mass migration on the part of the Regulators. After Turner's rebellion the slave code was made harsher, dozens of innocent slaves were lynched, and slavery was more deeply entrenched as an institution than before. The most immediate and important results of the battle at Homestead were the entry of the militia and the facilitation of the introduction of strikebreakers, which rendered the strike appreciably easier to defeat. The forays against the mines after the battle at Ludlow had no evident connection with the modest improvements in the lot of the miners that did result from the strike. In all four instances there was no decrement in violations of moral principles by the oppressor that can legitimately be attributed to the violence of the oppressed. Hence the violence of the oppressed cannot in any of these instances be justified as an instrument of social change.

However, it might be argued that without the violence of the oppressed, the conditions they were obliged to endure would have been even worse than they actually were. Violence might be justified, then, not as bringing about improvement in conditions but rather as preventing deterioration in them. This is a valid argument. But in the four cases there is simply no evidence to be found that the violence of the oppressed did in fact have the effect of preventing a deterioration in conditions. If anything, violence may have encouraged the oppressor to believe that he was justified in turning the screw.

Again, it might be argued that it is unfair to expect the oppressed to have been able to have estimated the outcome of their resort to violence beforehand. The criterion should instead be whether the oppressed had some reasonable grounds for expecting their violence to succeed in the circumstances that existed before they made their attempt. It is unfair for us with the advantage of hindsight to expect the oppressed to have foreseen exactly where the vicissitudes of violence would lead them.

This argument, too, is valid, and correctly states the standard of judgment that should be applied to the agent who resorts to violence for purposes of assigning blame. But that is not what I have done. I have instead sought to assess the rightness or wrongness of the actions of the oppressed. Were they justified in the circumstances? In asking this question, hindsight is relevant. If the justification of an action is supposed to be that it results in social change, then it is highly relevant to know whether it did in fact have this effect, and there is no point in not taking full advantage of all presently available knowledge in determining whether the action did after all turn out to be justified on this ground.

I am driven by these considerations to the conclusion that in none of the four historical episodes can the violence of the oppressed be justified as an instrument of social change. Nor, I am further arguing, can unsuccessful violence ever be justified in restrospect on this ground. This is not an argument based on considerations of prudence. The point is that to be morally justified violence for the purpose of social change must succeed in producing that change. If it does not, we are left with the undoubted maleficence of the violence done by the oppressed, and we are left without any compensatory diminution in the violation of moral principles by the oppressor.

Violence for the purpose of social change is inherently a

very risky enterprise because the oppressed in their weakness can rarely literally coerce the oppressor. Yet if change
is what is to justify violence, and the responsibility for that
change is actually the oppressor's, then the oppressed in
doing their violence put themselves morally in hock to the
oppressor. Violence is a ploy of the weak. Like every other
tactical device to which the weak may resort, violence is not
likely to succeed. But from a moral standpoint, violence
has the peculiar disadvantage of being inherently wrong
because it is harmful and destructive, often terribly unfair
in its incidence, and is dangerously liable to get out of control and go further than was intended or can be justified.
Now if the wrongness of violence is to be justified by the
compensatory right in which it results, it must be recalled
that typically it is expected that that right, if it is done, will
be done by the oppressor himself. The rightness of what
the oppressed do is thus made to depend on a choice made
by the oppressor on what is in actuality his own responsibility. Typically, he will make the wrong, the immoral,
choice. When he does, the justification of the violence of
the oppressed as an instrument of social change is undermined. If the violence of the oppressed is ever to be justified, it cannot be so on this shaky ground.

   In ascertaining the extent of a decrement in injustice
accomplished by violence, or, in other words, in evaluating
how successful violence has been, it is useful to distinguish
two sorts of objectives that the oppressed may try to reach
by means of violence. Tactical objectives are those such as
forcing the Pinkertons or Governor Tryon's troops to surrender or retreat, Turner's killing as many whites as possible, or the Colorado miners destroying mine buildings and
equipment. A less immediate but still essentially tactical

objective was seizing the arms in Jerusalem. A borderline case was creating sufficient disorder to oblige the federal government to send troops into southern Colorado. The second sort of objective is strategic; these have already been mentioned frequently: to put an end to the charging of extortionate fees and pocketing of tax money, to gain freedom from slavery, and to make employers give up a share of their autocratic control over terms of work. A strategic objective is one that results in ameliorating the maleficent conduct of the oppressor. A tactical objective is what violence can directly attain by main force—death, destruction, injury, damage, and behavior forced by fear of these consequences. The crucial moral distinction between these two sorts of objectives is that only the achievement of strategic ends can serve to offset the maleficence of doing violence to others. Moreover, the scoring of tactical successes entails doing harm, and generally the greater the success, the more the harm done. (The possible successful use of mere threats of violence complicates matters.)

In all the historical cases except the Battle of Alamance, some degree of tactical success was achieved. (And even the Regulators, by means of the nondeadly violence at Hillsborough, had earlier gotten a few months' respite from taxes and courts.) In each of these cases it is difficult to see how the success actually achieved or a still greater degree of tactical success could have brought any closer the strategic objection sought. Even if Turner had succeeded in seizing any arms in Jerusalem, he would still have come hard against the disorganization and accommodationist attitude of the black community, confronted by militant, outraged and powerful white adversaries. The strikers at Homestead outfought the Pinkertons and forced their surrender—a complete tactical success of no strategic value whatever, if not a strategic setback. The all-day battle was taken to demonstrate the need for the intervention of the militia, a step inimical to the interests of the strikers.

The case of the Colorado Coal War is complicated by the strikers' success in getting rid of the brutally oppressive regime of the state militiamen and the company's guards, both in fact hirelings of the employers. Although removal of this regime was not the purpose of the strike, it became an important strategic objective of the strikers, particularly after the Ludlow Massacre. It would be unrealistic to contend that anything less than widespread, organized, and costly violence would in the circumstances have induced the president to send in the army. But it is possible to draw a distinction between the deaths of mine guards largely incidental to efforts to get access to mine property so it could be destroyed and the deaths attributable to vengeful and bloodthirsty desires on the part of the attackers. All accounts of the attacks after the massacre agree that much of the killing was of the latter sort, and if it was, it can only be regarded as wasteful.

More important, the ultimate strategic objective of the strikers in Colorado was not the removal or replacement of the militia, but rather recognition of their union. The deadly violence of the militiamen at Ludlow engendered publicity and pressure that eventually led the company to make at least marginal improvements in conditions in the mines. The workers' violent response to the militia's violence did not generate favorable publicity, and the massacre by itself would probably have led to the investigations and criticism of company policy that eventuated in the formation of a company union. It seems, then, that the minimal reforms in which the strike did result are attributable to the pressures generated by publicity about the Ludlow Massacre and may well have come about more in spite of than because of the strikers' own violence.

In general, the violence of the oppressed in the four cases seems to have been tactically at least partially successful and to have been strategically a complete failure. On the scales of moral assessment the degree of tactical success is but a measure of success in violating the principle of nonmaleficence. Only strategic success can serve to offset the moral failure implicit in tactical success.

In conclusion I want first to provide some general reasons for taking the skeptical position that I have about the efficacy of deadly violence, then to approach the problem of efficacy in a more general and perhaps sophisticated fashion again to show that skepticism is well warranted, and finally to reject two false inferences that might be drawn from my views.

Perhaps the main thrust of my argument has been to say that if one looks in some detail at a few cases where deadly violence was in fact used by the oppressed, it can be seen rather clearly that it simply did not work and hence that skepticism about its use in other similar situations is well warranted. But it is important to note that when I speak of violence "working" I do not mean to deny that violence may rather frequently succeed in satisfying the intentions of those who choose to use it as a means to achieve their ends. I take no position on this proposition. I make instead the narrower claim that deadly violence undertaken by or on behalf of the legitimate interest of the oppressed only infrequently succeeds in significantly advancing those interests. I try to show simply that this was in fact the case on four occasions in American history when it might more

plausibly than on most other occasions be asserted that violence did indeed work in this narrow and special sense.

A priori considerations buttress this finding of an historical survey. Those who are oppressed are by definition
weak and powerless. In a sense this assertion holds true
even for a revolutionary situation, since if a class is so
strongly situated that it can take over the reins of government it must by then be possessed of sufficient social resources as no longer to be considered oppressed. The weak
and powerless are possessed of very limited resources with
which to resist the will of their oppressors. It follows that
any attempt to resist by resort to deadly force is a priori
likely to prove futile and wasteful. It is plausible to suppose that more restrained and appealing tactics that play
on the sympathies of more powerful third parties and
conscience-stricken oppressors are more likely to be effective than deadly violence, but it would be sentimental to
suppose that there is always something effective that the
oppressed and their sympathizers can do to lighten the
former's burdens. Sometimes nothing effective can be done,
except perhaps to gather resources and lay plans for some
future contingencies.

Aside from the lessons of experience and the implications of the meaning of the concept of oppression, a third
reason for being skeptical about the justifiability of the
deadly violence of the oppressed is the certainty of its immediate, undesired effect and the relative uncertainty of its
desired, long-term effects. With a modicum of competence
and luck, any genuine attempt to kill should succeed in
taking life. But whether killing will then result in improv-
ing the oppressive conduct of others is much more uncer-
tain, as it depends on a change of heart in men presumably
rather brutal and hard-nosed or the mounting of coercive

power by men presumably weak and ineffectual. The certainty of evil (the taking of life) must be weighed against the problematic prospect of a lessening of the weight of oppression imposed by men presumably immune even to many of the pressures of other powerful men who are more or less their peers.

On a straightforward utilitarian view, a more sophisticated approach to these issues is possible. We could stipulate that the expected utility of the outcome of the action requiring justification be multiplied by the probability of its occurring. Using this approach, we could rather plausibly justify the very resorts to violence I have argued are unjustified. This is most obviously true in the case of a revolt against slavery, since presumably we should have to assign a very large utility to freedom. If we then make good a claim that there was at least some appreciable chance that the violence would succeed (for instance, that the Turner rebellion would cause the Virginia legislature to undertake a program of emancipation and stick to it—an implausible but perhaps conceivable prospect), even a fairly low probability multiplied by the very high value of freedom should result in a rather large value to be set against the disvalue of the loss of life.

It is obvious first of all that this approach to this sort of moral question can in practice prove to be highly dangerous. Those who are prepared to kill to achieve an objective will naturally tend to place a very high value on it, quite likely a higher value than a more objective observer would think warranted. It is equally apparent that, as already argued, a retrospective judgment of the justifiability of violent actions has no need to deal with merely probable outcomes but can instead take advantage of all the knowledge hindsight affords. But a deeper and more interesting objection to this line of reasoning has been well put by Lawrence H. Tribe in an essay on some modern techniques and principles of problem solving. Of perspectives that focus exclusively on the end results of social processes, assuming the maximization of some desired end to be the very essence of rationality, Tribe remarks that they exhibit "no independent concern for the *procedure* whereby those outcomes are produced or for the *history* out of which they evolve." Such a perspective is significantly distorted because "In most areas of human endeavor—from performing a symphony to orchestrating a society—the processes and rules that constitute the enterprise and define the roles of its participants matter quite apart from any identifiable 'end state' that is ultimately produced. Indeed, in many cases it is the process itself that matters *most* to those who take part in it."[18] What must be weighed against the desirable outcomes deadly violence may produce is not only a quantum of fatalities but also the terror the prospect of killing may induce, the mistrust it engenders, the bloodthirstiness it encourages, and the propensity it promotes to regard other persons as being subhuman. These are all features of the processes of violence themselves, and not merely outcomes of such processes. There is no place for these considerations in any simple calculus of utilities and probabilities.

I wish finally to deny the validity of two possible objections to my argument that may at first sight seem plausible. The first is that it constitutes a prescription for quiescence, for acquiescent acceptance of whatever outrage the oppressor may choose to perpetrate against his hapless victims. This is simply untrue. For one thing, on my argument deadly violence may be found to be justifiable whenever it does in fact promise to bring about a sufficiently significant improvement in the conduct of the oppressor and on other grounds as well. For another, there usually exists a very wide range of alternative means of resistance other than deadly violence and, what is equally important, this range encompasses most of the forms that the resistance of the oppressed has in fact taken over the centuries. An argument narrowly concerned with deadly violence says nothing about these alternative forms of resistance, and its implications may be rather latitudinarian if the taking of life is regarded as being substantially more serious than the destruction of property and the oppression of other persons.

The second charge that might be leveled at the argument is that it is too pragmatic in character and equates success with morality. This is not true. Part of the argument asserts that the chances of "success," that is, inducing the oppressor to improve his behavior, can scarcely be irrelevant to an attempt to justify what must be presumed to be an immoral act, the deliberate taking of a human life. Surely lightening the burdens of oppression is the justification that a resister who resorts to deadly violence would in fact put forward if he were called to account for what he has done. What is alleged to be pragmatism is in fact merely the modicum of responsibility that any moral agent must exhibit as long as he is at all concerned to justify his actions on moral grounds. If he is not so concerned and wishes to argue that his admittedly immoral act is justified by some other, nonmoral considerations, then at least it will be plainly apparent that he has chosen simply to ignore the binding force of moral considerations. He can do so, but he cannot then honestly assert that what he is doing is the morally right thing to do. Yet most persons who resort to deadly violence in fact do wish to make this claim, and when they do, they base their case on the improvement of the conditions of those persons on whose behalf they have behaved with such extreme maleficence. And this, as we have seen, is from a moral standpoint inherently a very risky enterprise.

3

Law and Revolution

In this chapter I intend to accomplish four objectives. The first is to give some indication of how lawyers approach the problem of the justification of homicide, a problem that seems on the surface to encompass the sort of issues we have thus far been considering. But the apparent ease with which the legal problem can be assimilated to those broader issues is highly misleading, and it is my second objective to show why this is so. I then begin the search for a more viable alternative approach to explaining why it is that the four cases of violence (Alamance, Homestead, Nat Turner, and Ludlow) discussed at length in this book are not so distinctive from revolutionary violence as they seem to be at first glance. My final objective is to show how the implicitly revolutionary character of the violence in the four cases suggests that a more adequate approach to the problem of justification than the legal one consists in assimilating it to the problem of the justification of revolution, a problem that in its turn rather resembles the problem of the just war. Some of the implications of this approach are drawn by way of introduction to chapter 4, in which criteria of justification of the violence of the oppressed are constructed.

Justification of Homicide

We are dealing in general with the question of what justifies taking of another's life. In other words, we are trying to establish standards for the moral justification of homicide. In this endeavor, it would be improvident not to make use of a well-established set of standards of justification that are impartially and judiciously arrived at and are founded on actual experience in a broad range of cases in which deadly force has been resorted to. Just such a set of standards is available in the statutory and customary law of human societies over the centuries. The law, we might note, embodies at least in the Anglo-American tradition the same distinction between justification and excuse on which I have placed heavy reliance. Legal excuses are pleas of diminished responsibility (ignorance, mistake, insanity) and usually result in reduced sentences. Pleas of justification assert or admit full responsibility and deny wrongdoing in the circumstances. If accepted, they result in a defendant's going free.

Yet there are also reasons why the legal standards embodied in the law of homicide are fundamentally dissimilar to those standards that are relevant to the problem of the violence of the oppressed. Legal standards provide an interesting sidelight on that problem, but they are not directly relevant to its solution. I therefore propose to ignore all the law of homicide outside the Anglo-American tradition, and even within that tradition to ignore the actual corpus of the law, both common law and statutory, and confine my attention instead to the *Model Penal Code* drawn up under the supervision of Herbert Weschler in the late 1950s.[1] Much more than the positive law, the code is based on explicit principles and is internally consistent. Moreover, it displays a deeper, more humane regard for the value of human life than the positive law does in most American jurisdictions, where the individual is well protected against the depredations of his fellow citizens, but not against the action of policemen and other agents of state authority.

Even the lives of innocent bystanders are placed in jeopardy by the weakness of existing restrictions on the use of force in apprehending and arresting suspected criminals. The *Model Penal Code* hews consistently to the sound principle that the police should risk taking life only when the lives of others or the police themselves are endangered.

Law Enforcement. I propose now to consider each of the main legal justifications of homicide in turn. One of these justifications is that force is required by the exigencies of the process of law enforcement. Force may well be justified in making an arrest, in preventing escape from custody, and in preventing the commission of a crime. The problems raised by each of these three steps in the process are essentially similar, so we can concentrate our attention on only one of them, making an arrest. To the use of force in making an arrest, the code would apply seven restrictions, only the last of which is controversial. The first requirement is that the force be necessary to effect the arrest. Other requirements are that the person making the arrest be authorized to act as a peace officer, that he make his purpose known if he can, and that, if he is acting under a warrant, the warrant be valid. The fifth requirement is that when deadly force is used, the arrest must be made for a felony and the sixth is that the force used should create "no substantial risk of injury to innocent persons" (*MPC*, p. 49). The seventh, and controversial, requirement is that the officer, when he makes use of deadly force, should believe "that there is a substantial risk that the person to be arrested will cause death or serious bodily harm if his apprehension is delayed" (*MPC*, p. 50).

The basic principle of this restriction is that life should not be taken except to preserve other life. When a person being arrested for theft runs away or an unarmed thief runs

away with his loot, he cannot under this restriction be shot
at by a policeman or guard. The penalty for theft is not
death; a trial might bring out mitigating circumstances,
and a higher value is placed on life than on property. For
these reasons, the thief is allowed to escape in the hope that
he will later be caught. The loss to the thief's victim can
be made up through such social mechanisms as insurance
and government compensation. Perhaps the victim's right
to possession of his property is impaired by a requirement
that the police let the unarmed thief flee rather than shoot
him, but the right to life that is the obverse of the natural
duty to abstain from deadly violence overrides the rights
of property.

Self-protection. We see later that because the policeman
has the same right to use force in self-protection as anyone
else, and as the obligation to retreat does not apply in the
same way to him as it does to other citizens, he has more
latitude in the use of force than restrictions on its use in
law enforcement make it appear he does. But before this
point can be explained, we have to consider the use of force
by the ordinary citizen to protect himself against the threat
of death. For the private citizen the criteria for the use of
deadly force to protect against death are three. The first is
that the citizen should believe "that such force is necessary
to protect himself." The second is that he should not, in
the same encounter, have "provoked the use of force against
himself . . . with the purpose of causing death or serious
bodily harm." The third, the so-called retreat rule, is that
it should not be the case that "the actor knows that he can
avoid the necessity of using [deadly] force with complete
safety by retreating or by surrendering possession of a thing
to a person asserting a claim of right thereto or by complying with a demand that he abstain from any action which

he has no duty to take." This obligation to retreat does not fully apply when the actor is attacked in his dwelling or place of work, but this qualification need not be considered here (*MPC*, p. 13).

I take it as a postulate that the law on self-protection against death embodies a sound moral principle. The point is an important one deserving elaborate argument. But for present purposes it will perhaps suffice simply to observe that we must take as given, *ex hypothesi*, that a situation exists where a life must be lost. (Were this not so, the criterion of necessity could not be satisfied.) The second criterion, concerning provocation, ensures that the responsibility for the existence of the dilemma of either violating the natural duty not to take life or losing one's own life falls on the assailant and not the person assailed. The reason for resolving the dilemma in favor of the person assailed is that the assailant created the dilemma. Both could live and would if the assailant had not taken the initiative in violating the injunction against doing violence to others. This injunction against violence properly applies only to persons who are innocent in the sense of not being a source of harm, and a person who endangers the life of another is not innocent in that sense.

The criterion of harmfulness is crude and often unfair, whereas the judicial standard of innocence is more humane and based on a wider range of considerations. Yet when self-defense is at issue these wider considerations are not relevant. Even if it is a child or a madman that endangers the victim's life, he is nonetheless entitled to kill in self-defense provided only that the criterion of necessity is satisfied.[2] If the taking of a life in self-defense is to be justified, the existence of the dilemma that a life has to be taken must be attributable to the person being defended against.

It does not follow that the person who created that dilemma must necessarily have done so in a way that makes him not innocent in the courtroom sense of that term.

The retreat rule seems to be a virtual corollary of the criterion of necessity. Any "necessity" not to retreat would have to arise not from the dictates of self-protection but from the moral imperative not to display cowardice and lack of manly conviction in the face of aggression. This brand of necessity will not do because, as has been stated in a classic treatment of the problem, "a really honorable man, a man of truly refined and elevated feeling, would perhaps always regret the apparent cowardice of a retreat, but he would regret ten times more, after the excitement of the contest was past, the thought that he had the blood of a fellow-being on his hands." [3]

Another and more plausible argument against the retreat rule is that it "cedes the field to any group of bullies prepared to make a show of deadly force." To this "the answer has been that the proper and sufficient remedy is not a trial of strength but rather a complaint to the police. If this foregoes a private sanction that might operate as a deterrent to aggressors, it does so in reliance on the adequacy of the public sanctions and does so only when the highest value is at stake" (*MPC*, pp. 24–25). It must also be recalled that the victim of protective deadly force may erroneously be thought to be an aggressor.

I remarked earlier that the peace officer has more latitude than the provision concerning the use of deadly force in law enforcement makes it appear. The peace officer's greater liberty derives from his being excepted from the retreat rule. If he is "justified in using force in the performance of his duties" or "in making an arrest or preventing an escape," then he "is not obliged to desist from efforts to perform such duty, effect such arrest or prevent such escape because of resistance or threatened resistance by or on behalf of the person against whom such action is directed" (*MPC*, p. 13). The need for such a provision is pressing. In its absence someone could avoid arrest simply by pointing a gun at the arresting officer and indicating to him a clear line of safe retreat. Once the obligation to retreat is removed from the policeman, his way is clear to use deadly force if he meets resistance that takes the form of deadly force—because he need not retreat, and on not doing so is faced with a threat that entitles him to use deadly force as a means of self-protection. It is not the process of law enforcement as such that opens the way to the use of deadly force, but rather the officer's standing his ground together with the decision of the person to be arrested to resist by means of force that endangers the life of the officer.

The limits on the policeman's use of deadly force are rather narrow. He may use such force only so as to protect the life of either himself or another. But if some other person attempts to resist him in the performance of his duties by means of deadly force, then the policeman need not retreat even if he safely can. Instead he must press forward and use whatever degree of force is necessary to carry out his duty. Resistance in the form of deadly force may justify his responding by using deadly force.

Protection of Others. Even someone unwilling to approve the use of deadly force in self-protection or in law enforcement might be unprepared to disallow the use of deadly force for the protection of other persons. The *Model Penal Code* provision on force for this purpose is derived from the provision on self-protection. The use of force against another person to protect a third person is said to be justifiable when "the actor would be justified under [the self-defense provision] in using such force to protect himself against the injury he believes to be threatened to the person whom he seeks to protect," and "under the circumstances as the actor believes them to be, the person whom he seeks to protect would be justified in using such protective force," and "the actor believes that his intervention is necessary for the protection of such other person" (*MPC*, p. 30). The retreat rule is modified similarly to fit the case of protecting another person.

Anyone who has dealt with the problem of pacifism, an absolute prohibition against the taking of human life, comes soon to realize how very difficult it is to defend an absolute view when the protection of other lives is at stake. If one abhors the thought of killing so much that he believes that he should let a homicidal assailant succeed rather than take his life, his belief is perhaps his privilege and his choice the preferable one as being noble and selfless. I would argue to the contrary that the deliberate sacrifice of one's own life to spare that of an assailant reflects a distorted sense of value and principle. But even if that argument cannot be made successfully, it is nonetheless very hard indeed not to conclude that a person who abstains from taking the life of one murderous individual when that is necessary to protect the lives of (several) other persons is himself failing to perform his duty to the killer's victims and is culpable for that failure. His failure may be based on conscientiously held principles, but the principles that would permit him to stand by passively when he could be saving the lives of other innocent persons must be seriously in error. The moral basis of this legal justification for homicide seems entirely firm. It is morally wrong to let innocent persons die so as to spare the life of their murderer.

Protection of Property. There is no provision in the

Model Penal Code that permits the use of deadly force for the protection of property as such. The nearest thing to an exception is the permission given to use deadly force against a person believed to be "attempting to dispossess [the actor] of his dwelling otherwise than under a claim of right to its possession" (*MPC*, p. 34). Weschler remarks that it is rare for anyone to attempt dispossession except under a claim of right, so that in the great majority of cases deadly force would not be justifiable. More to the point, the basis for the narrow exception that is allowed is not the value of a dwelling as a piece of property, but rather the reasonable fear for one's own safety that breaking in without a claim of right engenders (*MPC*, p. 39). Even if one feels that the code makes too large a concession to tradition, it is still true that the principle that property is never to be valued more highly than life is not breached, or at least that no principled defense of such a breach is permitted.

It is important to note that the self-protection provision can come into play in circumstances other than an assault coming out of the blue or arising in the course of a quarrel. The code states that a person must, if he can, avoid the necessity of using deadly force "by surrendering possession of a thing to a person asserting a claim of right thereto or by complying with a demand that he abstain from any action which he had no duty to take" (*MPC*, p. 13). A robber cannot and does not assert a claim of right. Therefore the "victim of a robbery may . . . refuse to yield his property," even though his refusal may well "precipitate a threat of deadly force." If the robber does react in this way, then the victim is free to "use equal force—not to prevent the robbery—but to defend himself" (*MPC*, p. 26). The result is perhaps not different from the prevailing privilege in many jurisdictions to use deadly force simply for the purpose of preventing a robbery as a way of enforcing the law that makes robbery a felony. But the rationale is significantly different. If deadly force can be used simply to prevent a robbery, then a greater evil (killing) is permitted to prevent a lesser evil (robbery). As the code reads, deadly force may be used only for self-defense, albeit the occasion for the need for self-defense is incidental to a refusal to comply with a robber's demand. The code is so constructed that whereas the privilege to use deadly force is limited to self-defense, this limitation does not imply an obligation to comply with a wrongful demand made at gunpoint.

Defense against Nondeadly Force. The *Model Penal Code* gives lip service to the notion that "the sanctity of life has a supreme place in the hierarchy of values" and that "in all ordinary circumstances lives in being must be assumed . . . to be of equal value" (*MPC*, p. 8). But these principles are not interpreted to mean what they seem to imply, namely that the taking of life can be justified in the protection of life and of no other value. Quite to the contrary, the use of deadly force is held to be justifiable when it is believed that it is necessary to protect against not only death, but also "serious bodily harm, rape or sodomy by force or intimidation, or kidnapping by violence" (*MPC*, p. 13). ("Serious bodily harm" is given a fairly precise definition: harm "which creates a substantial risk of death or which causes serious, permanent disfigurement, or protracted loss or impairment of the function of any bodily member or organ" [*MPC*, p. 82].)

The reason for these further exceptions to the prohibition against homicide might conceivably be that they all involve some risk of death and hence justify the taking of life on that account and not for their intrinsic characteristics. But if this were the rationale for additional exceptions, then the provision would have to read differently than it does, since in some instances bodily harm, rape, or kidnapping are much more life-threatening than in others, in some few scarcely at all, and it would be unfair not to give due consideration to the degree to which these offenses endanger life. The language of the comment on this provision ("There is no complete agreement on the nature of the extreme harm against which it is permissible to defend oneself by the use of deadly force" [*MPC*, p. 21].) strongly suggests that a contrast is intended between "extreme harm" and "deadly force," and that the former need not be tainted by the latter for homicide to be justified.

It is reasonably clear then and of some interest that even within the confines of law the use of deadly force for some purposes other than the preservation of life is permitted. But is the law morally lax on this point? Does it perhaps make concessions to man's baser nature rather than require the forbearance that a reasonable morality would demand? These are important and complex questions, but for the purposes of the analysis in this chapter there is no need to try to answer them. Instead let me conclude by observing that a legal approach to the problem of the justification of the deadly violence of the oppressed does not give the proponents of such violence much comfort. The provision concerning self-defense promises to be most useful to them, but in at least two of the four cases such a defense could not get very far. The attacks on the mines in southern Colorado and the homesteads of southern Virginia were clearly aggressive in character, however severe the provocation to which they were a response. The strikers at Homestead first opened fire on the Pinkertons while they were still in the middle of the river a mile downstream from the mill, and they also took no advantage of the opportunity they had to retreat safely. The retreat rule also offers substantial difficulties to an attempt to justify on legal grounds the Regulators who took the field at Alamance.

The legal justifications we have examined here are not entirely useless or inappropriate in trying to determine whether the deadly violence of the oppressed is morally justifiable. If such violence satisfied legal standards of justification, it would probably be morally justified as well. And we can easily imagine trials for murder being conducted in any of the four historical cases (with the possible exception of the Battle of Alamance). Trials for murder actually occurred in Pennsylvania, Colorado, and Virginia. But in trials for homicide where there are many actors trying to do harm, severe evidentiary problems arise in attempts to assign responsibility for whatever fatalities occur. The law is not particularly well suited to solving problems of this kind. As Sanford Levinson has remarked:

There seems to be an inverse relationship between the number of individuals involved in a transaction or event and the efficacy of traditional legal analysis as a mode of comprehending it. Once beyond a strictly two-person interaction—be it a murder, contract, or automobile accident, we enter the world of respondeat superior, agency, aiding and abetting, or conspiracy law. Even that law loses its power as anything more than a formal analysis when the individuals involved pass beyond a small number. And of no area is this more true than criminal law.[4]

The weakness of the grip of the law on the sort of violent acts with which we have been dealing is attributable to factors that lie deeper than evidentiary difficulties and multiple actors. A more fundamental weakness of the law as the basis for an evaluation of these acts is that the ordinary sort of homicide that the law is designed to deal with is normally intended by the agent to remove some obstacle to the attainment of essentially private ends—a guardian or possessor of money, the companion of an attractive woman, a destroyer of pride or reputation, or an informant capable of putting the agent in jail. Or the ordinary murderer may act chiefly to vent his rage and hatred by destroying the life of any person he happens to encounter. In any case, the agent's motives and purposes differ fundamentally from those of the agents in the four historical episodes where men killed for essentially public ends—to remove obstacles to the rearrangement of political and social conditions. Specifically, they strove to convert an extortionate tax system into a fair and reasonable one, to preserve or create relations between management and labor based on bargaining and mutual agreement rather than autocratic and unilateral decree, and to transform slave labor into free labor. Their goal, as described in chapter 2, was to cause their oppressors to cease behaving in accustomed ways. But at the level of social description, their goal was to secure the abolition or redefinition of certain social roles and systems of relations. Killing in these four situations was intended to remove (or, on the other side, to keep in place) obstacles to a socially defined goal.

Suppose that an agent involved in one of the four situations wishes to act justly and rightly and is called on to take up arms to further the cause of the oppressed. In deciding on the course of action to take, a relevant and important— but by no means decisive—consideration to be weighed is the severity of the injustice to be remedied. (Other considerations have to do with the efficacy and necessity of violence in achieving the righting of injustice.) Thus a very important consideration in justifying the violence of the oppressed is the severity of the injustice of oppressive social and political conditions. Yet despite the central importance of such a consideration, it must be noted and emphasized that the law cannot admit it and assign it its due weight and importance. Such a law would have to read something like, "homicide is justified when intended to rectify unjust conditions existent in our society." But a law reading like this would be a very odd one for any legislator to assent to. Presumably each legislator is himself committed to rectifying any unjust conditions existent in his society. Presumably also he would support the measures necessary to rectify unjust conditions if a citizen went no further than to point out the existence of such conditions to the members of the legislature. So it seems that a law reading like the one just quoted would imply that: (1) certain unjust conditions exist or may in the future come to exist, (2) those in the legislature intend to do nothing about them, at least until such time as the conditions provoke violence on the part of those victimized by them or their sympathizers, and (3) hence others may act, in violent fashion, to improve the conditions complained of. Thus if a legislature added to the statutes a clause declaring that homicide in the interests of the alleviation of unjust social conditions was permissible, it would be implicitly abdicating its own responsibility to alleviate unjust social conditions. This would be a very strange action for a legislature to take.

It might be argued in favor of such a strange action that deadly violence should be permitted either as constituting an unusually effective way of alerting the legislature to the existence of unjust conditions or as a device by which it will become politically feasible for the legislature to take effective action when this would not otherwise have been possible. But surely quite dramatic ways of seeking attention might be imagined that would not be so costly and reprehensible as the taking of human life. The argument about political feasibility appeals to the fact that in circumstances where the law does not contain the exception to the prohibition against homicide that is being considered, violence does occasionally induce legislators to take action that they would not have taken otherwise. But assuming the exception was put into the law, when would the presence of unjust conditions be decided on, and by whom? The answer can only be, under the constitution of present-day states, by the courts during a trial. The courts will decide whether a defendant was correct in his belief that unjust social conditions existed and justified homicide to bring about their removal.

Now clearly the sensible thing to do rather than permitting homicide in these exceptional cases would be to set up a special court—we might call it a "court of the outraged" —that would take only cases in which the plaintiff alleged the existence of conditions so unconscionable as to justify homicide and where the state defended the conditions. The court would have the power either to determine that such conditions do not exist or that they do and to order or recommend appropriate remedies. The chief disadvantage of a "court of the outraged" over a court that tried actual homicides is that it would have an extremely crowded docket. Its advantages are that it does not require the plaintiff to risk punishment for homicide should his estimate of the conditions that outrage him be adjudged incorrect and that it protects all citizens against being killed by the outraged.

The addition to the customary defenses against a charge of homicide (self-protection, protection of others, prevention of crime, etc.) of a new defense, the alleviation of unjust conditions, thus appears to be if not logically impossible, at least a very odd sort of action for a legislature to take. Hence the underlying rationale of the homicides for which the oppressed were responsible in the course of the four episodes seems to be one that cannot possibly be accommodated by a legal code. If these acts are to be justified, it must be on moral, and not legal, grounds. If they do happen to be legally justifiable, then it must be for reasons other than their having the peculiar characteristic of having been done in the course of an effort to rectify unjust conditions.

If legal justifications are not appropriate to the violence of the oppressed, can a more sensible framework of justification be found? I believe that the most useful analogue is revolution, and that the four situations have more in common with revolution than what appears at first glance. The justification of revolution can in turn make good use of the standards developed in the literature on the just war, in spite of the important differences between war and revolution.[5]

Justification of Revolution

One may be tempted to reject the analogue of revolution out of hand as irrelevant to the more trifling cases of violence we have considered here. But this would be a serious error, as I now try to show.

"Revolution" has been variously defined. Merely for purposes of illustration, let me cite three concise and useful definitions. The first is adapted from Eugene Kamenka: "We [consider] as a revolution any sharp, sudden change or attempted change in the location of political power which involved either the use or the threat of violence and, if successful, expressed itself in the manifest and perhaps radical transformation of the process of government, the accepted foundations of sovereignty or legitimacy, and the conception of the political and/or social order." Another, by Sigmund Neumann, defines a revolution as "a sweeping, fundamental change in political organization, social structure, economic property control, and the predominant myth of a social order, thus indicating a major break in the continuity of development." A more recent definition, especially applicable to twentieth-century revolutions, is given by John Dunn:

Revolutions are a form of massive, violent and rapid social change. They are also attempts to embody a set of values in a new or at least a renovated social order. . . . Revolutionaries are committed by their proclaimed beliefs to changes not only in the tenure of positions of power but to changes in the social stratification (in some cases even to the eventual disappearance of any such social phenomenon as social stratification), to drastic improvements in social welfare and eventually to decisive changes in ideology (that is: not merely in the ritual proclamation of those political and social values which it is physically prudent to proclaim, but to a transformation in the way in which men's experience of living in their society leads them to perceive and to feel about that society).[6]

Now it would be possible to work through these and other similar definitions and arrive at a set of criteria that define "revolution." The criteria might be necessary or even sufficient conditions for a historical event to be called a revolution, or more sensibly, they might be considered a set of conditions of which many or most must be present for an occurrence to be a revolutionary one. Still more soundly, they might be regarded as a list of the kinds of concrete, detailed, empirical data that suggest a phenomenon is revolutionary in character. But rather than deal with

definitions derived directly from historical experience, I
want to attempt an a priori theoretical approach that I expect to permit the construction of a definition that will
incorporate the standards of the Kamenka–Neumann–
Dunn sort of definition and serve also to arrange them in
a coherent and theoretically illuminating way.

The theory—if that is not too pretentious a term—that
I apply here is one propounded by W. G. Runciman. The
main idea is that all human societies are stratified—not
merely differentiated—along three dimensions, and that in-
vidiousness is inherent in being positioned high or low on
any of these dimensions. (Thus, for example, having more
or less education is not inherently a good or bad thing, except as education makes a difference in one's place along
one or more of the three dimensions.) The three dimensions are the familiar Weberian ones: (political) power,
(economic) class, and (social) status. In describing how a society is stratified it is necessary to ask, as Runciman does,
"three separate kinds of question: first, who is more and
who is less advantageously placed in the system of production, distribution and exchange? second, who is more and
who is less highly regarded by the fellow-members of his
society in terms of social prestige? third, who is and who
isn't in a position to coerce or induce other members of his
society into doing what they would not otherwise do even
when they are averse to doing it?"[7] The key point is that
differences that lie in those three dimensions must be invidious, and that all invidious social distinctions can be
placed in or reduced to one of these three dimensions.

If this theory is valid, as I assume it is, then its applica-
bility to the problem of defining "revolution" is apparent.
Revolution is a process that drastically relocates many
people some distance along one or probably all three di-

mensions of inequality. Relocation along the three dimensions thus supplies three possible criteria of revolution. An additional three criteria may be that such relocation or change be over some considerable distance, involve many people, and be accomplished by violent or illegal means. A seventh and more complex criterion has to do with the "decisive changes in ideology" to which Dunn refers or what Neumann terms "the predominant myth of a social order." I think it arguable that this sort of change may be an epiphenomenon of change in social structure, but I nonetheless give consideration to this factor as an independent criterion.

With a serviceable definition of revolution in hand, let me now discuss whether the four incidents of violence sketched in chapter 1 are incipiently and implicitly revolutionary. I do not argue that the perpetrators of violence in these situations intended revolutionary change. Instead, I hold that from an objective standpoint, lifting from their shoulders the oppressive conditions that caused their sense of outrage and indignation would have required changes that largely satisfy the definitional criteria of revolution. The rebels in the four cases in seeking freedom from oppression unwittingly but necessarily sought to bring about changes revolutionary in their scope and intensity.

Few would be inclined to doubt the implicitly or even overtly revolutionary character of one of the cases. This, of course, is the slave uprising in Southampton County. Clearly, if the slaves became free men and full citizens, a massive redistribution of political power would have occurred. Moreover, the very small proportion of the white community that owned the greatest share of all slaves would have been stripped of its power by the effective enfranchisement of southern blacks. To strip this class of its property without compensation would destroy the upper class of southern society, and emancipation would also cause many changes in the relative economic standing of more middling slaveowners. These changes would entail great shifts of relative social status and the shattering of the myths of in-born inequality, social hierarchy, and aristocratic virtue that were part of the foundations of southern society. "Slavery," Eugene Genovese remarks, "established the basis of the planter's position and power. It measured his af-fluence, marked his status, and supplied leisure for social graces and aristocratic duties." In addition, "The road to power lay through the plantation. The older aristocracy kept its leadership or made room for men following the same road. An aristocratic stance . . . was the soul and con-tent of a rising power."[8] The slave who sought freedom for himself and his fellows necessarily sought revolution throughout the South. That legal emancipation meant not freedom but a new form of servitude is not to the point; what the slave—and then the tenant—wanted was freedom, and freedom for him, at least if suddenly and violently attained, meant revolution for southern society.

That the Regulators of North Carolina implicitly strove for revolutionary ends is less clear than in the case of the slaves of southern Virginia. But on reflection it is hard to see how they could have attained freedom from extortion-ate local rule without a sharp redistribution of political power away from the local oligarchy into the hands of both the provincial government and the local populace. As Bas-sett shrewdly remarks, the only practicable way of achieving local fiscal reform was the exercise of strong supervisory powers by the provincial executive. And had this centrali-zation of power come about, it would have occurred in response to the demands of the small farmers of the North

Carolina Piedmont. Such unprecedented responsiveness would have been symbolic of a revolution in the accountability of government to the people and a substantial enhancement of popular control over government. Similarly, the ending of anxiety-ridden dependence on the arbitrary caprice of depradatory and uncontrolled oligarchy would have constituted in effect a revolution in the class structure of Piedmont society. It is hard to envisage such extensive changes in social relations not being marked also by changes in the predominant ideology that would lend greater emphasis to the responsibility of the local oligarchs to attend to the public welfare and conform to some rudimentary standards of justice. Indeed, the new ideology that would have accompanied or given impetus to new social relations might even have been fundamentally democratic in character. The cessation of extortionate fiscal practices that was the Regulators' immediate aim may fairly be said to have entailed or required further changes that aggregately amounted to a revolution for those affected.

We come now to the two cases of labor violence, Homestead and Ludlow. Here the central demand of the oppressed was nothing more far-reaching than recognition of a union, which may seem scarcely a revolutionary demand. Yet I think further exploration of these events will yield a good deal of support for the thesis that had the strikers in these incidents got what they wanted, a revolutionary shift in political, economic, and social relations would have come along in tandem. If all the miners of southern Colorado and steelworkers of America count as "many people," then I would think it at least arguable that all seven criteria for the definition of revolution are met by both cases, although I am somewhat more certain about Colorado than

Pennsylvania. Let me turn first to the situation in Colorado, which I think is fairly clear-cut.

We might begin by noting that the subjective view of the mineowners was consonant with the notion that revolutionary stakes were at issue in 1914. One historian comments that "many of the coal operatives believed their system was fundamental and necessary. They were sincere in their fear that union organization would spell the end of business enterprise and individual freedoms of the type cherished by boards of directors. Their psychology was not unlike that of the ruling class of a monarchy of a kingdom of a century ago." John D. Rockefeller himself exemplified this attitude. Asked why he had done nothing to end the killing, he replied: "We believe that the issue is not a local one in Colorado. . . . It is a national issue of whether workers shall be allowed to work under such conditions as they may choose. And as part owners of the property, our interest in the laboring men of this country is so immense, so deep, so profound that we stand ready to lose every cent we put in that company rather than see the men we have employed thrown out of work and have imposed upon them conditions which are not of their seeking and which neither they nor we can see are in our interest."[9] No slaveholder could have been more retrograde, condescending, and obtuse. More to the point, one of the parties to the conflict in Colorado saw the stakes as being of revolutionary proportions.

A more objective reason why the Colorado case seems implicitly revolutionary is the substantial evidence available that Colorado was, for those of its citizens who happened to do manual labor for the Colorado Fuel and Iron Company, not a democratic state but a business-run autocracy. First Amendment freedoms were effectively denied not only where men tried to discuss organizing the union but even in the schoolroom, in church, and at the newsstand. The company manipulated and controlled the ballot itself by measures extending to outright fraud and corruption when these were deemed expedient. This unjust and unjustly maintained concentration of political power was used to continue the economic degradation of the worker, who was obliged to drink typhoid-infested water, rent company-owned hovels and shacks, shop at high-priced company stores, work under hazardous conditions, and generally live on a subsistence level in abject dependence on the good will and caprice of the company.

If a strong union had gained the power to bargain on a give-and-take basis with a company that so dominated the economic and political life of its workers, would not the transformation in the political power, economic standing, and social status of its membership and the reciprocal decline in the authority and perquisites of management have been sufficiently great to be considered revolutionary in extent? It seems to me apparent that they would, that the pride and sense of well-being, the economic independence and political assertiveness of organized workers who had beaten the company and forced it to bargain with their representatives as at least formal equals could only mark a profound break with the past that deserves to be called revolutionary. The point seems especially well taken when we recall that a complete collapse in social control was manifest throughout the strike region after the Ludlow Massacre and until the introduction of federal troops. No revolution was accomplished, but the incumbent regime proved in the end utterly incapable of carrying out the functions of government. Were it not for the federal presence, Colorado could after Ludlow have been governed only by chaos or by a union-dominated coalition government. Its rule might have been precarious and temporary, but in the Colorado case not only was a revolution requisite to the liberation of the oppressed, but for a brief while the collapse of social control that must precede or that constitutes a part of any revolution actually occurred.

The Homestead case is more complicated in part because available sources lack any evidence that Frick and Carnegie dominated the Pittsburgh region politically as Rockefeller did southern Colorado, and in part because Frick and Carnegie set out to break a union that was already well established rather than to prevent a fresh attempt at unionization. At Homestead it was Frick and Carnegie who accomplished a revolution by reversing more than a decade of substantial progress under the leadership of a strong and healthy, albeit conservative and exclusive, union. Evidence adduced in chapter 1 makes evident, I think, that the workers of the Carnegie empire who had occupied a decent and respectable place in the economic life of the region were suddenly cast into roles of abject dependence and unaccustomed squalor. After 1892 came the seven-day week, together with the twelve-hour day and a twenty-four-hour shift every two weeks; there were also secret wage scales, the elimination of extra pay for Sunday work, and reductions in pay to levels far below those before the strike.

Together with this reversal in economic well-being went denials of political rights and economic prerogatives. Grievance committees were abolished and workers were simply forbidden to meet at all. An elaborate spy system was set up and a miasma of apathy, mistrust, rivalry, and degradation settled over the community. Where once the power of organized and unified labor had stood against the power of management, now nothing stood in the way of two or three dominant men ruthlessly determined to extract every penny of profit they could from the company, whatever the human cost.

Since the workers at Homestead sought merely to preserve the strength of their union and the status quo in general, it is odd to say that they implicitly or otherwise sought revolution. Yet it does seem that Frick and Carnegie were trying to set the calendar back and to transform for the worse the conditions of workers at Homestead. The transformation they succeeded in bringing about in the economic and social status of the workers was so marked and its effects on the political morale of the workers so debilitating that the stakes at Homestead may have been no lower than in many situations all would agree to be plainly revolutionary. At Homestead the workers were resisting a loss in status, power, and economic well-being that bids fair to be considered revolutionary in its proportions, except that revolutions are by definition regarded as being equalitarian and progressive, and the breaking of the union was a backward and oligarchic step.

I conclude that a close look at the four cases reveals them to be implicitly revolutionary, or nearly so. I believe that this conclusion is buttressed when we consider how the convergence between revolution and rebellion may also be seen from the other side. Recent scholarship[10] and for that matter a bare recounting of the facts—the restoration of Charles II, Thermidor and Napoleon, collectivization— tend to show how surprisingly little the lot of the oppressed has been improved by the great revolutions. More important, such improvements in their economic, political, and social standing as are accomplished often come about with a minimum of deadly violence. (The acquisition of land by the French peasant, for example, was largely accomplished without bloodshed.) Taking the discontinuous transformation of economic, social, and political conditions that the rebels were in each case implicitly demanding of their oppressors, as well as the uncertainty of the assumption that the great revolutions have themselves fully met the rigorous criteria of Neumann, Kamenka, and Dunn, we may reasonably conclude that the four situations are not so distinctly nonrevolutionary as they may appear at first glance. Probably what distinguishes a revolutionary situation from the likes of the four cases dealt with at length in this essay is not the radical character of the transformation social justice required, but rather the scale of the hopes aroused and the strong sense of the possibility of sweeping change that have characterized the great revolutions. Perhaps these hopes and expectations themselves create new men who forever are actors of a new and more demanding sort on the political scene, but perhaps also they are more delusional than we are wont to allow.

An important inference to be drawn from the implicitly revolutionary character of these relatively minor incidents of violence, an inference that reinforces a central theme of this essay, concerns the enormity of the strategic task that faces the oppressed. The inferior location of the oppressed on the dimensions of political, economic, and social inequality is a vital prerequisite to the justification of a resort to violence on their part and at the same time constitutes a position of weakness from which attempts to improve that position are inherently unlikely to succeed. The denial of a just share of societal resources that is the source of a legitimate sense of outrage also renders an attempt to improve conditions difficult to accomplish. This is a conun-

drum that confounds virtually any attempt of the oppressed to alleviate their condition by their own efforts.
And just as the condition that leads to violence on their
part is likely to be especially outrageous and hence possessed of great justificatory force, so also is that same condition likely to be marked by a lack of resources so pro-
nounced as to doom a resort to violence—and indeed most
if not all other feasible methods of redress.

The implicitly revolutionary character of the four incidents serves to remind us, though it does not imply, and
the failure of the legal approach strongly suggests, if it
does not imply, that it will not do to regard the decision to
kill in the cause of justice as one taken by an isolated individual in relation to other isolated individuals. Rather
we will do better to analogize the killing that occurred in
these minor incidents to two other sorts of killing engaged
in by groups of human beings and often regarded as being
quite justified in certain circumstances, namely, revolution
and war. Indeed, these two deadly social activities are far
from dissimilar in the logic of justification applicable to
each. One reason for this similarity is the fact that, as remarked by John Dunn, "revolutionary seizure of power
(as opposed to intraelite *coups d'état*) usually in the twen-
tieth century [and also in the great revolutions in England
and France of the seventeenth and eighteenth centuries,
respectively] takes place by means of protracted civil
war."[11] The chief difference between the two sorts of combat thus becomes that the one is international and the
other intranational. War is a conflict between two sov-
ereignties; in revolution, sovereignty is "up for grabs
within a specific social and political entity."[12] The stakes in
the one case are the international structure or balance of

power and in the other the sort of domestic arrangements a social and political entity is to have.

However, from a moral standpoint the stakes are not as different as they seem. For the preservation of national security can scarcely be a value worth killing and dying for, except as the domestic arrangements of a nation are worth securing. The reason for fearing foreign conquest and occupation is presumably that foreigners are, and usually rightly, regarded as being incapable of ruling others of a different language or culture with the sensitivity and responsiveness to their needs and wants that justice requires. Even the worst possible outcome of a war, occupation, is not from a moral standpoint worth killing to prevent unless the domestic arrangements that result from conquest are worse or are less subject to future change than those that existed before the war.

I would conclude then that the morally crucial objective of both war and revolution is to change the social, political, and economic conditions under which a group of people are to be obliged to live. Given the nature of this objective and given further that the killing is being undertaken not by isolated individuals against other isolated individuals, but rather by members of social groups who intend to or will bring about significant social change, it becomes clear that the question confronting the individual is not only whether or not to *kill* but also whether or not to *join*. The choice is, if you will, rather like that of the voter faced with supporting one of two alternative regimes. So also is the citizen caught up in an armed rebellion sometimes obliged to choose the sort of society in whose creation he wants to participate.

The armed rebel is importantly unlike the voter in that

he violates the principle of nonmaleficence by joining either side. It may seem then that he can keep his hands clean by abstaining from joining either side. Yet to make this choice may be to violate the principle of justice. And as soon as one moves from the individual to the social plane of analysis, it can be seen that even the principle of nonmaleficence is not necessarily best served by abstinence from combat. Assume that one's goal is to minimize the number of lives lost in the course of a conflict. Imagine now a hypothetical band of a thousand "death-minimizers" pledged to take whatever course of action will result in the loss of as few lives as possible. It is obvious that their optimum strategy will not in all circumstances be to sit the fight out. They might sometimes do better to join the losers to prevent their suffering a particularly bloody defeat or series of defeats. In other circumstances they might do best to join the winning side so as to shorten the war in a way that reduces the total number of fatalities. War is after all an enterprise in which maleficent conduct can honestly and rightly be judged to produce less bloodshed than does refraining from maleficence. It follows that even the principle of nonmaleficence taken by itself is not an easy one to apply.

The problem becomes still more complex when the principle of nonmaleficence must be weighed against the principle of justice. In chapter 4 I construct five criteria for determining when a resort to violence is justifiable. The first and fifth of these can be largely derived from the principle of justice and the other three, from the principle of nonmaleficence. In the interplay of the five criteria derivative from these two fundamental principles lies the answer to the question of what is to be done.

4

Criteria of Justification

In this concluding chapter I want to summarize the foregoing argument by setting out five criteria that must be
satisfied for the justification of those among the oppressed
or their sympathizers who resort to deadly violence. I take
it that all five criteria must be satisfied and that failure to
meet any of them will render a violent undertaking morally
insupportable. I also assume that other unstated criteria
must be satisfied and that while those I consider include the
ones of greatest importance, they are not themselves sufficient. The five criteria I set out are rather similar to and
often derivative from the many similar lists of criteria established in justification of civil disobedience, but they are
necessarily much more demanding than those for breaking
the law in a civil fashion. This greater restrictiveness is
requisite because civil disobedience narrowly conceived is
an exercise in persuasion entirely respectful of the rights of
others, whereas a resort to violence necessarily invades the
rights of others and imposes costs that tend to be coercive
on other members of the community.

In seeking to establish the validity of the criteria I have
settled on I want to make use, in rudimentary fashion, of
the device employed by John Rawls in his theory of justice.[1] Rawls argues that the principles of justice, that is, the
principles defining "the way in which the major social institutions distribute fundamental rights and duties and
determine the division of advantages from social coopera-

tion" (Rawls, p. 7) are those principles that would be devised in a certain way. They would be those principles devised by rational men (in the sense of the term employed in welfare economics) who are free of envy and who want to advance their own interests (Rawls, pp. 143, 147). Such men might settle on biased or unfair principles, but they are constrained to devise the principles from behind a "veil of ignorance." They know the general facts about human society, psychology, and sociology. But they are ignorant of the particular circumstances of their own society and of their own individual place in it, their conception of the good, their natural abilities, their psychological quirks (Rawls, p. 137). This very thick veil makes all men equal in a very deep sense.[2] From this position of equality, "the original position," the principles determining the political constitution and the economic and social arrangements of society are to be devised. This position is a certain point of view that anyone can adopt at any time (Rawls, p. 139). The principles that would be chosen from this perspective are the principles of justice.

Rawls contends that two basic substantive principles would be chosen in the original position. The first concerns liberty. "Each person is to have an equal right to the most extensive total of liberty for all." The second concerns economic justice. "Social and economic inequalities are to be arranged so that they are both: (a) to the greatest benefit of the least advantaged . . . and (b) attached to offices and positions open to all under conditions of fair equality of opportunity" (Rawls, p. 302). All key terms in these principles are given a more precise and elaborate sense by Rawls, but the first principle is an idealization of freedom of conscience and freedom of speech and the other freedoms essential to the workings of popular rule and the exercise of individual rights, whereas the second principle forbids discrimination and requires the reformation of society to overcome the effects of financial, educational, and emotional deprivation, and further to redistribute economic resources so as to maximize the welfare of the least advantaged.

This is a very brief summary of a very complex theory. I propose to adopt it to my own uses in a very simplified way so as to arrive at principles of an order lower than Rawls's more important ones. I imagine "rational contractors" seeking to arrive at the criteria controlling the resort to deadly violence in a way analogous to that in which Rawls's contractors arrive at criteria controlling the resort of civil disobedience (Rawls, pp. 371–77, 382–91). Despite its vulnerabilities, an approach of this sort provides a relatively objective and dispassionate standpoint from which standards of conduct can be devised. This standpoint is also a profoundly egalitarian one.[3]

The Criterion of Injustice

The first criterion for the resort to deadly violence must obviously be that something has gone awry and needs to be put right. The rational contractors would always reckon that life lost might be their own and would not permit this prospect without good reason. We now need to state more precisely the nature of the something gone awry that can justify resort to violence. Its nature can best be seen by making use of the theory of morality advanced in 1971 by David A. J. Richards. Richards's theory is an extension of the Rawlsian device of the original position from the realm of social justice to all of social morality. Whereas Rawls centers his attention on the institutional principles of equal liberty and distributive justice, Richards goes further by formulating principles of fairness (which he takes to include fidelity, veracity, and gratitude), of individual duty (nonmaleficence, mutual aid, consideration, paternalistic guidance), and of "supererogation" (civility, mutual respect and love, beneficence). More ambitiously and dubiously, he also tries to show that in the original position men would assign to these dozen or so principles an invariant lexicographical ordering. Richards's fifth principle is that of nonmaleficence: "persons are not, intentionally or knowingly, to be cruel or to injure . . . or kill persons, except for cases of necessary self-defence." But this principle comes into play only "given that principles 1 and 4, as applied to and between basic legal institutions, and the economic and social institutions they define and support, are satisfied or not relevant." Principle 1 is one of the principles Rawls derives from the original position, the principle of equal liberty—in Richards's formulation, "Basic institutions are to be set up and arranged so that every person in the institution is guaranteed and secured the greatest equal liberty and opportunity compatible with a like liberty and opportunity for all." Principle 4 concerns fairness, in that when

an existent institution makes its beneficiaries better off than they would be with no such institution and also satisfies the equal liberty requirements of principle 1, then persons who voluntarily accept the benefits of such cooperative institutions, and depend on others to do their part when it comes their turn to bear the burdens involved in sustaining the institution, are themselves to bear such burdens, when it comes their turn. . . .

[Moreover,] persons are to advance and promote the existence of institutions which satisfy the principles of justice [i.e., Rawls's two principles], given that this involves little cost to such persons.[4]

Of course both Richards's formulation of the principles and the order assigned them are open to dispute. I would myself reject the strictness of his lexicographical ordering. But the crucial point is that, as I will try to show, Richards is correct in stating that the principle of nonmaleficence generally comes into full play only after some of the principles that determine the basic institutional structure of society have been satisfied.

At the outset it should be made clear that the priority assigned to the principles of justice over the principle of nonmaleficence is not to be taken to mean that the way is open to wanton killing. It means rather that some constraints on killing presuppose the presence of just institutions and that unjust treatment makes killing permissible as a way of restoring and creating more just institutions. But it may nevertheless seem odd that rational contractors would open the way to any killing whatsoever. Would they not prefer physical survival on any terms to the risk of finding themselves cast in the role of oppressor and killed as a consequence? Is not life the supreme value, surpassing even justice?

One indication that it may not be is given by the fact of our admiration of a man who lays down his life for a cause worthy of such a sacrifice. His making the sacrifice of his own volition importantly distinguishes the case from that in which the lives of others are taken against their will, but it does suffice to show that from a moral point of view life is not always the supreme value, and it has added force since those rebels who take the lives of others usually risk

their own in so doing. But we have yet to confront squarely
the issue of whether the loss of life can be outweighed by
the value of what can roughly be called liberation from oppression, meaning the restructuring of social arrangements
in a significantly more just way. One reason why a rational
contractor would value liberation over life, to adopt a
crude and perhaps misleading shorthand expression, is that
the scope of injustice—the number of victims at a particular time and over one or several generations—may well be
substantially greater than that of most deadly violence.
More pointedly, in the original position the choice the
contractors will have is one between some risk of death at
the hands of those who rise up against oppression and some
risk of themselves being victims of oppression, which may
be a heavy weight to bear. Typically the scope of oppression is greater than that of violence by a wide enough
margin that the latter risk is significantly greater than the
former. But even if this is not true, a rational contractor
might still prefer liberation to life. One reason for this
preference is to ensure that at least those occupants of oppressive roles who have wittingly and willingly undertaken
to play them would be put on notice of the risk they run
in so doing, and to ensure further that the victim of oppression would be morally at liberty to free himself despite
scruples to the contrary. A second and more fundamental
reason is that unjust social arrangements stunt and deform
the lives of their victims by denying them the liberty and
opportunity to enjoy fully their innate skills and powers.
The truncation of potential human development is not
murder, but it is a blight and waste of what a person might
become. A rational contractor would fear the prospect of
stunting and deformation no less than death itself, at least
so long as the risk of the former was substantially less than

that of the latter. Hence the principles of justice take precedence over even the principle of nonmaleficence.

We must still say with some degree of precision what the nature of the injustice or wrong that should be incorporated in the first criterion is. The suggestion made by Rawls in his consideration of civil disobedience is that the injustice to be invoked should be "substantial and clear" and that instances of it should preferably be limited "to those which block in the way of removing other injustices" (Rawls, p. 372). More specifically, this would restrict "civil disobedience to serious infringements of the first principle of justice, the principle of equal liberty, and to blatant violations of the second part of the second principle, the principle of fair equality of opportunity" (Rawls, p. 372). The denial to a minority of the right to vote and hold office and the repression or denial of opportunities to a certain religious group are instances of the sort of injustice Rawls has in mind.

For the special case of deadly violence I would propose a less abstract criterion of injustice in line with the preceding reference to the arrested development of the personality in which social injustice results. If the grave difficulties connected with making sense of the notion of a potential person can be overcome, then we could say that the stunting or deformation of this person is tantamount to murder and that only when it occurs can deadly violence possibly be justified in response. The main idea here is that injustice can truncate human development as surely as deadly violence can end physical survival and all the other elements of personhood, and that when the more subtle and indefinable form of destruction occurs, deadly violence can with the satisfaction of further criteria be an appropriate means of bringing it to an end.

As I said earlier, the notion of potential persons is difficult to comprehend. What are we to make, for instance, of the man who had the potential to be either a violinist or a mathematician and who snuffed out the one potential to develop the other? But I do not think it worthwhile working through these problems or devising some alternative means of assessing the severity of the injustice or wrong referred to in the first criterion. This is so because nearly all societies throughout history have been rife with injustice that anyone with a modicum of vision and sensitivity could easily become outraged by. Even the maldistribution of income that Americans regard as being as fixed a part of the social landscape as the Rockies are of the natural landscape can easily be seen as a totally unnecessary, personality-stunting species of injustice. In particular cases it is of course important to establish with certainty whether the first criterion has been satisfied, and very frequently men who resort to violence do so with only a semblance of justification. But of all the five criteria I consider, this is the most easily satisfied.

It is satisfied, that is to say, in the sense that it is easy to show that severe injustices are present in almost any society, though they are often not felt or believed to be unjust. The mere existence of unjust conditions is not itself sufficient evidence that violence is an appropriate response to their presence. But it is interesting to note that grievances justificatory of violence occur rather frequently in most societies. Prior to the late nineteenth century, most citizens of what is now the industrialized world were denied even the most elementary of liberties, the right to vote. Although the franchise is today virtually universal in most countries of a western European heritage and in Japan, disparities of power in the workplace are excessive, and power is unduly

irresponsible in the larger polity. So also are existing inequalities of wealth and income indefensibly large.[5] It is
not difficult to conceive of drastic reallocations of economic resources and political power as being morally imperative because they effectively constitute the denial of equal
liberty or fair opportunity that Rawls says may justify illegal action, and in extreme situations disruptive and even
violent actions.[6] In any event, few would wish to dispute
that slaves are victims of a very substantial injustice, and it
seems equally clear that victims of governmental extortion
in prerevolutionary North Carolina and of de facto tyranny
in the mining country of Colorado in 1913 also could fairly
assert their situation satisfied the first criterion. A strong
argument to the same effect can be made for the workers of
Homestead. The general conclusion I draw is that the first
criterion is in itself not a very restrictive one and that some
men in most societies across the years can legitimately claim
that their grievances satisfy it.

The most natural way to construe the first criterion in
relation to the others is to take the righting of a substantial
injustice to be an "end" and to take violence to be the
"means" of achieving this end. Such a construal is highly
misleading, for it assumes that the end (righting injustice,
creating new social and political conditions) is fixed, unaf-
fected by the nature of the means used to bring the end
about. As we saw at the end of chapter 2 and as Antony
Flew has clearly shown, this assumption is false. Whether
slaves are liberated (and masters deprived of their "property") by peaceful or violent means, whether extortionate
tax collectors are removed by force or otherwise, or whether labor unions gain recognition in response to violence or
to other inducements makes a difference not merely to the
means described but also to the specific nature of the end

accomplished. Moreover, the practice of violence may have a strong effect on those who employ it. Men who have steeled themselves to kill on even one occasion, let alone over a long campaign of random terror and cruel reprisal, are unlikely to emerge from their experience as the same men they were before. Nor is their movement or organization likely to be quite the same as one otherwise similar but consistently nonviolent. The righting of injustice performed by men who have engaged in programmatic or even episodic violence will not be the same business as performed by those who have avoided violence. Whether the effect on ends of violent means is a desirable one is beside the point; violent means do not leave ends intact. The larger and more important point, well put by Flew, is

that we should not imagine that to lead a moral life is primarily . . . a matter of achieving or attempting objectives, and that to find in any given situation what one ought to do is a matter of finding a way to bring into being some positive good. [Such a belief is at best misleading. Rather] to do one's duty . . . is rarely if ever to achieve . . . an objective. [Instead] it is to meet, or to find a way to meet claims; and also, of course, to eschew misdemeanors. Promises must be kept, debts must be paid, dependents must be looked after; and stealing, lying, and cruelty must be avoided.[7]

Furthermore, it is misleading to accentuate the positive in trying to understand the object of morality. "Our primary duties," as Flew says, "are to fulfill fairly specific obligations and to assist in the removing of definite evils. If we do have any general duty to promote happiness or any other positive good, this duty is certainly always much less important than that of preventing suffering."

To summarize and conclude, "the first question for the

moral agent must always be deontological. . . . The teleo-
logical, utilitarian questions about consequences arise only
when there is a conflict between accepted rules, or when
the acceptability of some present or proposed rule is at
issue." [8]

Flew's argument, though less far-reaching than Tribe's,
adopted in chapter 2, is open to objection. For one thing,
in admitting of a duty "to assist in removing definite evils,"
Flew may seem to open a large loophole if my own view that
most societies are shot through with consequential injustices is well taken. Is not unjust economic deprivation, for
instance, a "definite evil" that cries out for removal? And if
the reply is the quite correct one that although such an evil
is indeed definite and damnable, its alleviation necessarily
entails large-scale social change of the sort Flew would clas-
sify as a general effort "to promote happiness," we are then
brought to the second objection, that the whole thrust of
Flew's argument is conservative and quiescent and must be
rejected as such by anyone who believes in social justice in
any but hypocritical fashion.

My answer to these objections will enable me to get on
the table some cards representing more or less empirical
notions about the efficacy of violence as a device for social
change. Let me begin by citing the wise counsel of J. M.
Cameron concerning both the ubiquity and the frangibil-
ity of violence:

In all human institutions, the family, the State, the school, and
in all great changes, there has been violence and we have absolutely no reason to suppose that violence will vanish if and
as we become more ingenious. . . . It is not always thought
either problematic or undesirable; and there may even be
about it a touch of the numinous, and its practice may be an

occupation for the devout. But in many cases violence will have about it the mark of failure. Where violence occurs there has been negligence or stupidity or a failure of intelligence and will.[9]

In the course of American history, the mark of failure has been about violence more than it has more civil methods of redress. As Richard Hofstadter has observed:

If violence sometimes works [on the whole more frequently for those who already have position and power than others], it does not follow that nothing but violence works. Most of the social reforms in American history have been brought about without violence, or with only a marginal and inessential use of it, by reformers who were prepared to carry on a long-term campaign of education and propaganda. The entire apparatus of the welfare state . . . is the achievement of active minorities which, while sometimes militant and always persistent, were also patient and nonviolent. . . . Such reforms were indeed long overdue. However, it does not follow that the use of violence would have hastened their coming. . . . The important element [in accounting for more rapid progress in Europe than in America despite there being less violence there than here] seems to have been not the resort to violence but the presence of powerful labor movements with a socialist commitment and the threat of sustained action through normal political channels.[10]

So my first empirical generalization is that in the industrial era in Europe and America violence has been on the whole inefficacious in bringing about human social reforms.

The second generalization on which I base my skepticism as to the efficacy of violence picks up on Hofstadter's remark that the violence that accompanies social change has often been "marginal and inessential." I believe that quite generally the violence that accompanies progressive and humane social change has been in and of itself nothing more than a mark of failure, a peripheral, detachable and regrettable excrescence on a generally healthy and effective political movement. I have already explained in some detail why I so regard the attacks launched by the miners against company property after the Ludlow massacre. The quarter loaf of reform the miners got in the end was attained more despite these gratuitous attacks than because of them. The massacre itself was more than enough to ensure that investigation, embarrassment, and reform would follow.

I would go further and argue that much of the violence of the oppressed in the course of the great revolutions was of a similar excrescent sort. One finds for instance that in the course of famous *journées* of the French Revolution when the Parisian crowd took to the streets, on only two occasions—the wholesale slaughter of the captured Swiss guards after the fall of the Tuileries palace on August 10, 1792 and the famous September massacres three weeks later —can the crowd be blamed for more than a handful of fatalities. And in neither of these cases can it be held that the slaughter was either necessary or even helpful to the cause of those who perpetrated it.[11] Even the Russian Revolution began relatively bloodlessly because of the political weakness of the regime and the élan and organization of the Bolsheviks. Except for the weeklong battle for Moscow, in which hundreds fell on both sides in a rehearsal for the civil war to come, the risings in the cities were remarkably bloodless affairs.[12] Even in Russia in November 1917 political factors played a preeminent role.

However, I do not wish to assert that deadly violence never has been nor can be put to humane and progressive purposes. Ted Honderich has stated the contrary point very strongly indeed. "The proposition that violence does as a

matter of fact promote progress toward freedom and equality in some circumstances can hardly be questioned. The
nostrum that nothing is gained by violence does not survive
a moment's reflection. It is remarkable, despite its service
to entrenched interests, and the amour propre of democratic politicians, that it persists at all." As is already evident,
I find Honderich's statement brash and overconfident, especially inasmuch as he himself concedes that "for the most
part" the violence of the oppressed fails to secure its objectives.[13] But suitably hedged about and qualified I can accept the substance of Honderich's assertion. One of the
ways in which I would qualify what Honderich has to say
is by indicating the form taken by deadly violence that *is*
effective in bringing about humane social change. I would
hold that such violence often, even typically, consists not in
mob violence, not in days of rage, not in spontaneous, fer-
vid outbreaks of popular outrage, but rather in set battles
fought by organized armies of trained and disciplined soldiers. The models I have in mind are the English Civil
War of 1642–1646 and the American Revolution, with the
exception of the guerrilla fighting endemic in the lower
South after the collapse of civil government late in the
war.[14] But a great many of the fatalities incident to the
French Revolution were incurred in the course of civil war
in the region of the Vendée from March to December of
1793. (Thousands more fell to the Terror after the insurgency had been broken, but that is another matter.) [15] And
the great bulk of the violence incident to the Russian Revolution occurred in the course of its civil war, although
unfortunately here again the Terror that followed the
bands of soldiers across the land may have been more deadly than the war proper, and less justifiably so.[16] It appears
that the violence most likely to be effectively put to pro-

gressive and humane ends is in the form of set battles between organized armies rather than the more inchoate
forms of violence where spontaneity and popular sentiment
play a more dominant role.

I do not mean to imply that all revolutionary violence is
humane and progressive in its effects. In this connection it
is worth noting that the interests ultimately served by revolutionary violence have not always proven to be those of
the segments of society that could most legitimately be described as "oppressed." The Levellers and their allies in the
New Model Army, the *sans-culottes* who instigated the Terror, and the peasants who made up the bulk of the Russian
populace in 1917 did not find their interests advanced to
the same extent as those of the landed and mercantile interests in Parliament, the bourgeoisie of revolutionary France,
and the Communist Party in Russia. Those who bore the
brunt of the fighting and did most of the killing and dying
did not always do so in their own interest so much as in
that of others in more dominant positions in society.

I have thus far ignored a whole genus of violence that
has since the 1930s been notably successful in freeing several countries—China, Vietnam, Cuba, Algeria, Mozam-
bique, Angola, and Guinea-Bissau—from reactionary or
foreign rule. Guerrilla war is the form of resistance adopted by those whose weakness forbids them to organize armies
to fight conventional warfare. Michael Walzer has argued
that the terror campaigns of successful guerrillas tend to be
reasonably discriminating—certainly more so than those of
the authorities—and that "under the circumstances, attacks
on local magistrates probably constitute legitimate warfare. Such men have consciously joined one side in a civil
dispute and presumably know the risks their choice entails.
They are, for all practical purposes, combatants." I am

skeptical of even this concession to the violent, since those chosen for assassination may well be the very officials who are most helpful to the people at a time when their suffering and deprivation may well be most acute. But I would concur with Walzer that "on the other hand, the arbitrary selection of hostages from unfriendly villages, the murder of suspects and 'class enemies,' the public administration of atrocious punishments . . . are illegitimate actions, inadequately justified by some underground version of the theory of military necessity."[17] And there still remains the question whether the replacement of one sort of tyranny by another provides sufficient justification for undertaking a guerrilla war in the first place. Perhaps foreign rule is always unbearably tyrannical, but sometimes the regimes that replace the foreigners are also tyrannical.

The Criterion of Prematurity

The preceding remarks apply in part to the other criteria of justification as much as they do to the first, and I now direct attention to them without further digression. The second criterion holds that violence should be eschewed if it is premature, that is, in the formulation of Gerald C. MacCallum, Jr., "if it is engaged in before less objectionable methods with reasonable chance of success have been tried." The criterion thus expressed is quite similar to the requirement that (here the formulation is Rawls's) normal appeals to the majority be made in good faith and have failed, or, briefly, that "the legal means of redress have proved to no avail." This is a much more sensible requirement than that legal means be exhausted, since, as Rawls suggests, "normal appeals can always be repeated." It suffices that "further attempts may reasonably be thought fruitless." Rawls goes on to make a further point, referred to at the beginning of this chapter, that is so relevant to the problem of the justification of violence that I quote it now in its entirety. He begins by stating that the condition of legal means having been exhausted before the bounds of legality are exceeded is only a presumption.

Some cases may be so extreme [he continues] that there may be no duty to use first only legal means of political opposition. If, for example, the legislature were to enact some outrageous violation of equal liberty, say by forbidding the religion of a weak and a defenseless minority, we surely could not expect that sect to oppose the law by normal political procedures. Indeed, even civil disobedience [which in Rawls's definition is a completely respectful and essentially harmless mode of address (pp. 366–67)] might be much too mild, the majority having already convicted itself of wantonly unjust and overtly hostile aims.[18]

One thing to be noted about Rawls's example is that while it is a case of substantial and clear injustice, it does not satisfy his own preference for injustices "which block in the way of removing other injustices." Members of a sect whose churches are shut down could presumably continue exercising the civil liberties of all other citizens in an effort to reopen them. In contrast, each of the four historical situations does provide an instance of injustices that impede the removal of others. As I have already tried to show in chapter 3, each of the four situations was one where change required what amounted, on a local scale, to revolution, and where democratic and legal alternatives to extranormal means of protest were not really available. Indeed, in any situation in which the first criterion is met it is likely that legal alternatives either will not be available or will be fairly soon run through and proven fruitless. The upshot is that the second criterion is like the first rather easily satisfied and that the difficulties of justification lie elsewhere. This point is illustrated by the fact that though the excrescent violence of the antiwar movement in the United States cannot be justified, it was scarcely reasonable by 1969 or 1970, if not earlier, for anyone fully aware of the horror of what America was doing in Indochina to give any but short shrift to a plea for *patience*. A completely persuasive case against resort to violence by the antiwar movement can be made, but it cannot be based on an untrue belief that American policy was not gravely in the wrong, nor that normal political appeals had not proven fruitless. It does not follow that normal political appeals in some form or other should not have been continued as the most advisable available alternative, nor does it follow that the tactics of the antiwar movement were the most effective that might have been devised. But whatever the failings of the movement, the normal political process itself had failed, as the tonnage of bombs dropped after the election of 1968 indicates. Nevertheless, those who would justifiably resort to violence have more than one or two hurdles to clear.

The resort to violence in each of the four situations can easily be seen to have satisfied the second criterion. The events preceding the Battle of Alamance perfectly illustrate the exhaustion of peaceable alternatives preceding a resort to violence. The slaves of Southampton County of course at no time had effective means of seeking redress of their grievances since they lacked all political rights. Only the apolitical and individualistic alternative of escape held out any hope at all. The attacks on company mines in southern Colorado were not undertaken prematurely, but rather were a direct response to the execrable Ludlow massacre;

their timing could scarcely have been more appropriate. Such was also the case at Homestead; granted the assumption that company men had to be excluded from the premises of the mill, the violence of the strikers was not premature but timely. Indeed, the occasion of the outbreak was the initiative of the Pinkertons.

Whatever the limits to the practical import of the second criterion, there is no doubt but that the parties to the original position would subscribe to it and that from this point of view its validity is not open to question. To make sense of prematurity as a separable consideration in resorting to violence, we must assume that violence can be presumed to prove effective more quickly than available alternatives. Thus the choice facing the parties is whether to be killed so that an injustice can be righted some weeks, months, or years sooner than it otherwise would have been or to remain in a condition of oppression for this added length of time. This way of structuring the choice assumes further that the means adopted will have no effect, or no adverse effect, on the end accomplished. As already explained, such an assumption may very well be false. But even if it is valid, the parties would still be inclined to conclude that the continuance of an injustice of long standing for a relatively much shorter period of time cannot justify the taking of the lives of others. A still more intractable problem is posed by the imposition of a new injustice, especially since quick action to remove it may serve to prevent its being set in concrete and not susceptible to effective opposition in the future. The best example we have seen of a newly imposed injustice not of long standing is the attempt by the management of Carnegie, Phipps and Company to break an established union. In this instance from a tactical standpoint the violence of the strikers was certainly not premature, and neither was it from a strategic standpoint, since the survival of the union as an effective force was indeed being tested by the strike. In this instance what we are inclined to say is not that the criterion of prematurity is an unsatisfactory one, but rather that in cases of newly imposed injustices it can readily be satisfied, because if violence is not resorted to in such cases immediately, it will never again offer any hope of being efficacious.

The Criterion of Gratuitousness

The third criterion for the resort to deadly violence is that such violence should not be gratuitous. Violence is gratuitous, in MacCallum's words, "if its contribution to success can be equalled by other, less objectionable methods." Such violence does make some contribution to success and can thus be distinguished from what MacCallum calls *promiscuous* violence, "that is, . . . violence or fighting that even in the view of the agent, would not contribute to success in preserving or attaining what he believes right."[19] The presence of success in prospect is thus assumed by the notion of gratuitous violence; some quantum of violence is permissible on this criterion, but not too much, not more than serves to bring success about.

As I have already argued in detail, the daylong battle at Homestead, at least after the offer of surrender, excellently illustrates a failure to meet this standard of judgment, regarding the events of the day as a tactical, shortrun situation and ignoring that in fuller perspective even the initial resistance to the Pinkerton's entry was ill-advised. In contrast, the rebels of the North Carolina Piedmont drawn up for battle at Alamance fully satisfied the criterion of gratuitousness and could hardly have done otherwise, prior to taking captives or forcing surrender, since they were in formal battle against combatants who offered a direct threat to their own lives and a source of armed resistance to the attainment of objectives.

The fighting following the Ludlow Massacre more closely resembled Homestead than Alamance. The outrage perpetrated by the hirelings of the company served by itself to bring about whatever success was attained; the attacks by the miners were in this respect redundant—gratuitous. Conclusions about Turner and his followers are harder to reach because of the difficulty of defining success in a tactical sense in their situation. If we assume the objective was to take control of any arms in Jerusalem, then a direct march on the objective makes most sense. If the stopoffs at the various homesteads along the way were necessary to gather more recruits, it is still not obvious that all the white women and children encountered had to be killed to prevent their spreading a warning—might they not have been bound and gagged instead? Perhaps the real point of all the examples except Alamance is that the criterion of gratuitousness is not often in fact satisfied by men who resort to deadly violence, because they exhibit a strong tendency to go further than the attainment of success demands. Further support for this conclusion is seen in the excesses of the civil wars in France and Russia in the course of their revolutions.

In the original position the contractors would adopt the principle of gratuitousness without hesitation since it concerns a sort of action that is inherently undesirable and *ex hypothesi* is unnecessary. The decision regarding the righting of injustice with or without unnecessary killing would not be a difficult one. The only complication that I can see arising in this connection is the possibility that killing of oppressors might be regarded as desirable as a means of righting the balance of injustice for which the oppressors had made themselves responsible. It would be easy to dismiss this argument out of hand as a simple plea for vengeance, but to do so would be to beg the question, since the argument asserts that killing is in this instance rightful, a form of retribution and not mere vengeance. An adequate but not very searching response to the argument may be that the parties to the original position would in any event wish to see such killing in retribution done only in accordance with the canons of due process of law. A more complete response is given later in a discussion of the Warsaw ghetto uprising.

As we have already seen, the criterion of gratuitousness presupposes the prospect of success. In some of the four situations, as in Colorado and at Homestead, tactical, battlefield success was in fact attained. In no case was strategic success, liberation from oppression, attained as a result of the deadly violence resorted to by the oppressed, and only in the case of the miners of southern Colorado was there any improvement at all in the condition of the oppressed. This suggests that the difficulties and obstacles faced by the oppressed were extremely formidable. For this reason we find our next criterion to be especially difficult to satisfy.

The Criterion of Wastefulness

According to this fourth criterion as stated by MacCallum, violence must not be wasteful. That is, "if, though [violence] is necessary for success, success cannot in any case be achieved because there is no chance of providing something

else also necessary," then it must be considered wasteful
and rejected accordingly. This criterion may appropriately
be compared to Rawls's condition of civil disobedience that
following satisfaction of the main criteria, which involve
the issue of moral justification, it remains to be established
that civil disobedience, though within our rights, is in addition wise and prudent. It would not be wise or prudent if
it, for instance, served "only to provoke harsh retaliation
of the majority." [20]

The point of this comparison with Rawls is to delineate
clearly the problems of civil disobedience and violence in
this regard. Civil disobedience, because it is respectful of
the rights of others and the stability of the legal system,
gives rise to no moral objections at all once it is established
that a substantial injustice has been done, that legal remedies have proven fruitless, and that the stability of the
legal system is not in jeopardy. Violence, however, may be
extremely objectionable even after these criteria have been
satisfied, because inherently it violates the (presumptive)
rights of others and does harm to their interests. Thus at
the juncture at which civil disobedience has been shown
to be no longer open to moral objections, violence only begins to satisfy the moral standards it must meet.

Yet there is no doubt that in the original position such
a criterion would be adopted. The choice faced there would
be between the prospect of being killed by violent actions
directed against oppression and the prospect of being a victim of oppression and remaining one despite the violent
actions taken. What would be the point of admitting the
possibility of homicides that serve no useful end?

Is there then nothing that can be said, under any circumstances, for rebellion for its own sake and for the sake of
inflicting some little damage, however slight, on the power

of the oppressor? A peculiarly painful and acute example of such rebellion was the uprising by the surviving inhabitants of the Warsaw ghetto in the spring of 1943. Their story can be briefly told. The resistance movement struck its first blow August 20, 1942, with an attempt on the life of a man believed to be the chief of the Jewish police. Other policemen, informers, and collaborators were assassinated. As a result of these slayings and, more important, the large number of deportations that began in July, the *Judenrat* atrophied and lost its power, to have its place taken by leaders favoring a policy of resistance.[21]

The uprising began when the Waffen-SS (*Schutzstaffel*, elite guard) surrounded and invaded the ghetto in the early morning hours of April 19, 1943. The resistance laid down enough fire that the Germans were obliged to withdraw that night to resume operations in the morning. During the next two days the Nazis made slow progress, gradually enlarging the portion of the ghetto under their control. After April 22 the situation deteriorated, with increasing numbers of Jews caught and killed. Inhabitants of the ghetto now began trying to slip out through the sewers. German engineers blew up the manholes and blocked off this escape. Only a few small bands of Jews were still above ground in the burned-out buildings; those in dugouts were buried in debris and suffocated. Corpses floated in the sewers.

On May 8 the commander of the Jewish forces was killed or committed suicide. German night patrols sent into the ghetto destroyed the remaining Jewish dugouts one by one. By May 15 shooting was sporadic, and on May 16 the battle was finished. Several thousand Jews were buried in the debris. More than fifty thousand surrendered. Seven thousand of these were shot; seven thousand more were transported to Treblinka; fifteen thousand were transported to Lublin;

the remainder were sent to labor camps. According to German sources, the Germans and their collaborators lost sixteen dead and eighty-five wounded. According to resistance sources, German fatalities exceeded one hundred. An operation the Germans had planned to complete in three days instead took nearly thirty.[22]

It appears that the best hope for the survival of some lay in the organization and supply of groups of young people to escape the ghetto and join nearby partisan units, at least wherever these units could be expected not to hunt refugees from the ghettos. Since such units did not exist until 1942 and as most partisans did murder escaped Jews, even this strategy held out little hope. The strategy also entailed singling out some for the chance of survival and denying it to others, as well as giving food and supplies to some at the expense of others. And it ran the risk of cruel retaliation under the doctrine of collective responsibility.[23]

Now the criterion of waste requires that success not be incapable of achievement because there is no chance of providing something else also necessary. What does this criterion imply about the actions of the underground Jewish Combat Organization in April and May of 1943? The crucial question is what is counted as "success." The armed resistance was marginally successful even as a means of self-defense. In looking at this aspect of the resistance, recall the distinction (further elaborated on at the end of this chapter) between two senses of "innocence"—innocence meaning "not harmful or dangerous," and "not morally culpable." Death as a penalty in retribution for wrongdoing can appropriately be visited only upon persons who are proven not to be innocent in the latter sense (if indeed death is ever an appropriate penalty). The levying of such a penalty cannot be just except as the result of a hearing in accord with the canons of due process. In the circumstances of Warsaw this requirement could scarcely be satisfied. Moreover, if it was to be satisfied it is doubtful that the Nazis and collaborators who happened to be killed in the course of the uprising would all have been found to be without sufficient excuse to have escaped the death penalty. Each may have had a story to tell in extenuation—a story of intimidation, ignorance, and adventurism. And even if one or all was a sadistic anti-Semite it is a fair presumption that higher-ranking personages beyond the reach of the guns of Warsaw were very much more blameworthy, giving rise to questions of equity if the killings are taken to be justified by quasijudicial standards.

Clearly the victims of the Nazis had no obligation to make the fine distinctions that determination of guilt or innocence in a judicial or quasijudicial sense, as the basis for determination of an appropriate punishment, would require. We must deal instead with innocence in the sense of not being currently harmful. Since the Nazis and collaborators who were killed had come to force the Jews into cattle cars bound for gas chambers, the only way the latter could escape was to break free of the control of their captors. An armed rising was the only way for even a handful to have a chance for freedom, and as in the confusion and fighting some few did break out and stay alive for at least a few weeks or months, the killing done by the Jews can be justified as a measure resorted to in self-defense. But as such it did not serve as redress or tip the scales of justice one way or the other. The victims of the Jews were not found guilty; they were merely discovered to have been thrown up as obstacles to freedom from a captivity that signified certain death.

Since the uprising confounded German expectations by

stretching a planned three-day operation into a thirty-day struggle that appreciably drained German resources, it may be justified in the same way as may the hundreds of other partisan raids and battles in Nazi-occupied territory. No government has been more deserving of armed resistance than the Nazis' and if this was true where German policy fell short of genocide, it was indubitably so in the ghettos of eastern Europe. Every weakening of German control and every diversion of German resources was a contribution to an extremely well-justified cause.

However, to allow that in April and May the underground scored a marginal success at self-defense or as a resistance movement is to say rather little. We have thus far ignored two salient facts about this resort to arms. One is that, as Lucy Dawidowicz observes, "when it became clear . . . that no option but death existed, the idea of resistance [became] an affective undertaking rather than an instrumental one. Scarcely any of the resistant young people seriously believed that resistance could save the remaining Jews in the ghetto, but all believed that by defying the Germans with whatever armed strength they could muster, they would redeem the honor of the Jews. Resistance was thus not defense in the sense that [organized defense against pogroms] had been. It was instead an act of desperation. . . . Since hope for survival had been abandoned, one must die gloriously." The second fact is that the members of the underground, in the words of one of them, "breathed with desire for revenge for all the crimes of our common foe." Among the victims, the passion for revenge was universal; "hatred for the Germans consumed them." One Jew wrote from Bialystok to Palestine, "We'll kill our slaughterers; they will have to fall together with us. . . . We call you to vengeance, revenge without remorse or mercy. . . . Vengeance! . . . Our scattered bones will not rest in peace, the scattered ashes of the crematoria will not lie still, until you have avenged us."[24]

In view of these facts about the motives and purposes of the members of the underground, did they "succeed"? In avenging themselves, only a little: even if the underground's estimates of German and SS casualties are the more accurate ones, the invaders' losses were small, and no one fell who had conceived or directed the policy of *Entfernung*. Nor is it really obvious what vengeance means or what the passion of the victims requires. As Michael Walzer argues, these passions and justice cannot be dissociated; passion can run wild, and justice can turn unfeeling. Walzer holds that "what we ask of ordinary Germans of the 1940s is not that they cringe in guilt before prosecutors and judges, but that they face the victims whom they couldn't or wouldn't help when it mattered and acknowledge the truth about what happened. That [Walzer thinks] is what the victims themselves would want, were they allowed to speak: not that all the Germans be 'wiped out,' but that they be required to confront the crime committed in their name."[25] Those who entered the Warsaw ghetto were not ordinary Germans; they were themselves the criminals. Yet even they may not be appropriately avenged by death. What the passion of their victims requires is justice, and where that lies is not in every case easy to say. However, what revenge requires and how it may be related to justice is not so central to the success of the Warsaw revolt as another question. To find the deeper significance of the killing of a few SS men and German soldiers in the spring of 1943, we must look to the "affective" aspect of that undertaking. Later generations have inherited a symbol and have seen erected a standard to which they may in a similar situation repair. But everything hinges not on the mere existence of an example, but rather on what that example consists in. What is to be done depends on what we understand was done.

What is exemplary about the actions of the young zealots of Warsaw? To understand, we must, as Walzer says, see the invaders in the eyes of their victims. We must see them "first of all in that frightening mirror, and only afterward in the light of a universalist morality and law." In the Warsaw revolt, when the circumstances are so clear and the crimes so awful, "that two-fold vision absolutely forbids forbearance." Today "justice must be done, for the sakes of the victims, on behalf of the victims, though in the name of everyone. It isn't revenge, but it is retribution—and wouldn't be just if it wasn't." [26] And then, when the fear and hatred was felt by the victim himself, what could he achieve by killing one of the accomplices in his own murder? Why was it preferable to die, in the words of one victim, not in "slow torment, but fighting"? Why should this little band "declare war on Germany—the most hopeless declaration of war that has ever been made"? [27]

To be successful, fighting must contribute to the preservation or attainment of what the fighter believes right.[28] What was right in Warsaw was, for one thing, that the victims not be kidnapped and murdered. These crimes were not prevented, except for a handful of escapees. What was also right in Warsaw was that the dignity and humanity of the victim's personality be preserved. Whether or not "a Gabriel Prosser or Nat Turner presents the opposite limiting case to the slavish personality" [29] (resistance and the resistant personality can take many forms), Eugene Genovese is right in stating that violent revolt is one way of defying and defeating indignity and exercising to the full the rights that the preservation and development of the personality require. The rebel Nat Turner did not and could not in every case kill a clearly identifiable agent of oppression, which is one reason to doubt whether he alone stands completely opposite Sambo. In Warsaw, every victim of the Jews was a kidnapper and an essential cog in a murder machine. Every victim stood squarely on the path to a place where the dignity and humanity of the prisoner could begin to be released and his very life preserved. If the prisoner was bound to die, it was only because of those who had placed themselves in that path. To exercise the most rudimentary of his rights and to preserve his life required that he move as far down the path as he could, by killing as many who stood in his way as he could. So long as he was armed and resistant, he was succeeding in eschewing submission to any indignity. The path away from certain death toward possible liberation he had every right to follow, and anyone who would use deadly force to stop him had to be overcome with deadly force. In this respect, the overcoming was an important sort of success.

As the closeness of my argument concerning even resistance to the holocaust makes evident, I regard the criterion of waste as being an extremely restrictive one, seldom satisfied by actual instances of the violence of the oppressed. In my view none of the four situations reviewed in some detail met this standard. Nor did much of the violence of the French and Russian Revolutions, for reasons given at the conclusion of the earlier discussion of the criterion of injustice. Those who are oppressed are weak and lacking in political resources. Hence it is quite probable that some, even many, of the conditions necessary to their obtaining freedom from oppression will be lacking. In these circumstances, which are typical and normal as well as outrageous, the oppressed are not morally at liberty to resort to deadly violence, even when no other accessible tactic will work at all. As long as they can do nothing effective, they are not at liberty to take action that will serve only to add substantially to the sum of human misery.

The Criterion of Legitimacy

Premature, gratuitous, and wasteful violence is objectionable because it is unnecessary or superfluous to the achievement of liberation from oppression. The fifth and last criterion I consider to be especially restrictive because it would forbid even some violence that is necessary and effective in achieving a measure of liberation. It provides that any violent means resorted to must remain within the bounds of legitimacy. The only kind of illegitimacy I discuss here is that consisting in harm done to the innocent, the notion being that violence, whatever its effectiveness, may not be permitted, or at least ought to be scanned with a jaundiced eye when it does harm to those who are not implicated in the injustice against which violence is directed. I approach this question by considering the remarkably clear and coherent, though not totally acceptable, analysis of Elizabeth Anscombe.[30]

Professor Anscombe's argument consists of three central theses. The first is that "The right to attack with a view to killing is something that belongs only to rulers and those whom they command to do it" (Anscombe, p. 45). Regarding the obvious counterexample of unauthorized violence in self-defense and defense of others, Anscombe says, "The plea of self-defence (or the defence of someone else) made by a private man who has killed someone else must in conscience—even if not in law—be a plea that the death of the other was not intended, but was a side effect of the measures taken to ward off the attack" (Anscombe, p. 45). So to shoot to kill, to set a lethal mantrap, and to lay poison for someone from whom one's life is in danger would be forbidden.

Anscombe's second thesis is a corollary or presupposition of the first: that "to think society's coercive authority is evil is akin to thinking the flesh evil and family life evil" (Anscombe, p. 43). "It is both necessary and right that there should be this exercise of [coercive] power [by rulers], [since] through it the world is less of a jungle than it could possibly be without it. . . . [O]ne should in principle be glad of the existence of such power, and only take exception to its unjust exercise" (Anscombe, p. 42). The last clause shows that Anscombe is not uncritical of the application of state power, which is not in her view always proper. Private violence is never acceptable; the state's use of force only sometimes is not. Unfortunately, Anscombe does not directly address herself to the question of whether the unjust use of deadly force may be met in kind by private persons. Presumably it can, but only when the intention that lies behind it is not to kill.

Anscombe's third thesis, the most important for my purposes, is that "the principal wickedness which is a temptation to those engaged in warfare [a form of violence conducted under the same authority as the application of coercive power by the state internally] is the killing of the innocent" (Anscombe, p. 44). Anscombe then proceeds to clarify the notion of innocence and noninnocence she is here employing. Noninnocence cannot in the midst of war be the finding of an impartial inquiry conducted in accord with the standards of due process because in warfare the sovereign authority that alone can conduct such an inquiry "is itself engaged as a party to the dispute and is not subject to a further earthly and temporal authority which can judge the issue" (Anscombe, p. 44).

A different conception of innocence must be found. "What is required," Anscombe argues, "for the people attacked to be non-innocent in the relevant sense, is that they should themselves be engaged in an objectively unjust proceeding which the attacker has the right to make his concern; or—the commonest case—should be unjustly attacking him. Then he can attack them with a view to stopping them; and also their supply lines and armament factories" (Anscombe, p. 45). But, Anscombe goes on to explain, mere farmers and textile workers, even when their deaths contribute toward victory, are not to be killed. "For murder is the deliberate killing of the innocent, whether for its own sake or as a means to some further end" (Anscombe, p. 45).

This notion of innocence gives rise to two central problems: (1) the practical matter of how the distinction between innocent and noninnocent ("doing harm" in the useful, precise, and notably restrictive formulation of Thomas Nagel)[31] can be accurately drawn or whether it is too loose and vague to be useful and (2) the issue of whether the prohibition against killing of the innocent can be maintained as absolutely as Anscombe would require. Another way of framing the second problem is to ask whether the loophole created in the principle of nonmaleficence by assigning greater priority to the principles of justice is to be so broad as to include innocent persons when the consequences of such a broadening would on the whole be for the best. The final clause is meant to refer to the sorts of utilitarian appeals that are advanced in support of the overriding of the prohibition of the killing of innocent persons.

The first of these central problems has been considered in an earlier chapter; the second is taken up now. It can be approached by asking the same sort of question that has been asked regarding the other criteria: would the taking of innocent lives be absolutely prohibited in the original position? But before turning directly to this central question, I should first explain why the parties to the original position would not in every case simply accept as binding the rule or principle that would maximize the number of lives saved in any given situation. Four examples drawn from an article by Philippa Foot[32] will, I hope, serve to clarify this point.

1. A riotous mob demands that a local judge put an innocent man to death on threat of the mob's running wild in a minority neighborhood and killing several others at random there (Foot, p. 387).

2. If an individual immune to a certain fatal disease is sacrificed, several patients afflicted with that disease may be saved by injection of the dead man's serum antibodies (Foot, p. 388).

3. A tyrant or madman threatens to kill or torture five innocent persons unless we kill or torture one (Foot, p. 389).

4. The lives of five patients in a hospital can be saved, but only by the administration of a certain gas, which would release deadly fumes into the room of another patient who cannot be moved (Foot, p. 392).

Each of the four examples shows that following the simple rule, "Maximize lives saved," sometimes has results contrary to our moral intuitions, and that the rule would not be adopted by the parties to the original position. They would instead agree with Anthony Flew that the general duty to promote any positive good is less important than the duty of preventing—and still more, not causing—suffering. Foot's analysis clarifies the application of this point in cases such as her examples. It is not true, she maintains, that "the size of the evil must always be our guide." Rather, "to refrain from inflicting injury ourselves is a stricter duty than to prevent other people from inflicting injury, which is not to say that the other is not a very strict duty indeed" (Foot, p. 392). In the original position the contractors would prefer a greater risk of merely dying to almost any risk at all of their being used as scapegoats or guinea pigs in violation of the fundamental right of every person to be treated as an end and not a means. We want our doctors, for instance, to do all they can to save us—but short of subjecting us to the risk of being deliberately killed even to save others.

Thus the principle of the protection of the innocent is sufficiently strong to foreclose the taking of life even to save life. But is it absolute? From the point of view of the original position the problem is not whether the principles of justice or the principle of nonmaleficence are to be given priority. Rather, the problem is that a particularly contemptible form of injustice (and not mere maleficence)— the killing of the innocent—is opposed to yet another injustice, oppressive social and political arrangements. Even if the killing of the innocent "works"—succeeds in righting injustice—a highly plausible case against the killing can still be made. The case against the killing of the innocent, even at the price of the continuance of unjust social arrangements, will rest not on a mere toting up of the number of corpses for which the unjust regime and the rebels against it were responsible, but rather on somehow weighing the magnitude of the injustice of the regime against the magnitude of the injustice of taking the lives of innocent persons to serve an allegedly higher end. In the original position the contractors would need to weigh, then, the risks of being victimized by either an oppressive regime or the random and likely terroristic violence of the oppressed.

Fortunately, the satisfaction of the second, third, and fourth criteria typically ensures that, as a practical matter, the violence of the oppressed will be directed against the noninnocent—the oppressors themselves and those who do their bidding. And fighters for freedom who freely kill those whom they allegedly wish to liberate or to let remain free of oppression are suspect when they promise just rule after they assume power. Those who kill the innocent when they are constrained by political weakness are not to be trusted when they attain power and face the temptations of freedom from the constraints of weakness. In any event, the injustice inherent in the killing of the innocent is itself so grave that only the righting of extreme oppression can justify it. To be blunt, the outright slaughter of innocent women and children is on its face worse than the injuriousness of all but the most oppressive of regimes. The only regimes that are undeniably sufficiently unjust to permit violations of the fifth criterion are those that deliberately take the lives of innocent members of the oppressed population. Thus the Jews of Nazi Europe could have ignored this criterion if the others were satisfied, and Irishmen might have been justified in terrorizing the people of London while the British regime in Ireland was deliberately permitting mass starvation there.

At Homestead and at Alamance, victims of oppression found themselves under armed attack and hence largely satisfied the criterion of noninnocence. One may query whether they were justified in taking up weapons and making a stand when and where they did, but certainly their victims were sources of harm until surrender had been offered. In southern Colorado some of those killed may not even have been armed, and even those who were and used their arms against the miners may well have done so under a legitimate claim of right. But the only one of the four cases in which the criterion of noninnocence is clearly unsatisfied, at least as far as *some* of the victims of the oppressed are concerned, is that of Nat Turner. Turner's confession, if it is authentic, and the evidence of the corpses put beyond dispute the contention that innocent persons were killed. Part of what Turner confessed was that "there was a little infant sleeping in a cradle, that was forgotten, until we had left the house and gone some distance, when Henry and Will returned and killed it." [33] Such a deed does not satisfy the criterion of legitimacy, nor is it a heroic ideal to be held up as a symbol for future generations.

My conclusions about the criterion of legitimacy as narrowly construed here are two. The first concerns the strength of the rationale underlying it. From the standpoint of the original position, a criterion of noninnocence seems especially persuasive. For its denial entails running the risk of being killed for no reason at all, of submitting oneself to a "rule of law" as exemplified at Kent State University. From that standpoint only the most efficacious of violence directed against the most oppressive, if not deadly, of regimes can even be tentatively considered to permit violation of the criterion of noninnocence.

The second conclusion concerns the restrictiveness of the criterion. The criterion seems not to be restrictive because only one of the four cases fails of justification on its account.

But this appearance of latitude is illusory. Many of the cases excluded from consideration on an intuitive basis as not being even plausibly justifiable lacked plausibility in large part precisely because they involved the taking of innocent lives. (A similar point can be made about the application of some of the other criteria to the four cases.) Furthermore, we should not forget that the "courtroom" sense of innocence, despite the manifest unfairness of holding those engaged in violence to it, and its consequent irrelevance, does not lose all its force as a moral consideration. It is a fact of violent conflict that the incidence of the fatalities in which it results is brutally unfair. Those who die in combat deserve their fate only by random chance. In an important sense, then, violence done without the protections of due process is bound to strike down the innocent. And even on a conception of innocence that is fairer to those who do violence, the natural tendency of violent men to kick the traces of the restraints of morality and rationality often leads to the victimization of those who are not currently sources of harm.

A Final Note

As one looks retrospectively at those historic occasions when the oppressed or their allies took up arms, he does not find a plenitude of cases in which the principles of chapter 2 or the criteria of chapter 4 were satisfied. Indeed, except for the War of Independence and the Indians' defense of their lives and well-being, the whole sweep of American history affords no readily identifiable instance of justifiable, unauthorized, and illegal homicidal violence. Even the War of Independence is open to some question regarding the criterion of injustice. An extensive and sympathetic review of outbreaks of violence in more than a century of French and English history also does not supply many instances of nonrevolutionary homicidal violence that satisfied the criteria established here.[34] One does find cases of justifiable violence against property; a particularly clear example is the attacks launched by Rebecca and her daughters in Wales during 1842 and 1843.[35] Other examples of justifiable violence against property can also be found. And the entire thrust of the argument of this essay serves further to buttress the defense of militant, persistent, but patient and nonviolent campaigns for social reform wherever this option is available.[36]

Yet the deadly violence of the oppressed is seldom justified under democratic conditions, and not easily justified even under tyranny. This normative conclusion rests in large part on an empirical generalization that, as Richard Hofstadter put it, "historically, violence has not been an effective weapon of the left, except in that rarest of rare circumstances, the truly revolutionary situation. Under normal circumstances, violence has more characteristically served domineering capitalists or trigger-happy police, peremptory sergeants or fascist hoodlums."[37] Hence a flat prohibition on unauthorized and illegal violence observed by all parties would over the years better serve the interests of the oppressed than those of the oppressor. In the terms of my own argument, the violence of the oppressed fails to satisfy the criterion of wastefulness because when the oppressed or those acting on their behalf resort to violence, certain conditions essential to its effective use are typically lacking.

What are those conditions? The objective of political violence is the redefinition of a system of (oppressive) social roles. The requisite conditions are those that enable or empower the oppressed to oblige the oppressor to modify or resign his role. Assuming the ineffectiveness of exercises in persuasion and appeals to conscience, the oppressed must seek either to impose intolerable costs on the oppressor themselves or to enlist the support of allies who can compel the oppressor to modify his ways. Deliberate, homicidal violence frightens potential allies and legitimizes suppression. Assuming the support of allies is indispensable to the success of the cause of the oppressed, it follows that the oppressed are sufficiently weak and exposed that they can be suppressed if they are deserted by their allies. Presumably it is the injustice of the conditions under which the oppressed live that has moved their allies to take up their cause. If the oppressed become killers, they do nothing to add to the injustice of their situation, and they make it appear that they are dangerous to anyone who refuses their demands; hence they cannot be trusted not to abuse the greater political resources they seek. Thus deadly violence does not seem a very useful way of attracting the support of better-situated political allies. (Terrorism may possibly serve to mobilize the support of the more wretched portions of society, but to add to their misery in the short run is an arrogant, callous, and morally risky course.)

The difficulty with the direct use of deadly violence as a means of resisting oppression is that ordinarily the rich and powerful can make use of their resources to employ more hired guns than the oppressed can hope to mobilize. They may hire them out of their own pocket, they may lean on the government to do their dirty work for them, or they may do some of both. But sooner or later, usually sooner, they can easily outgun and outman the oppressed. When this is not the case—when conditions begin to approximate "that rarest of rare circumstances, a truly revolutionary situation"—the most vital and important conditions for the success of the oppressed will *not* be their possession and use of sheer physical force. Rather, the conditions crucial to their success will lie in new social and political arrangements already in being, and a new ideology already prevalent, of which effective physical force is more a result than a cause. Given the existence of these new arrangements and the prevalence of a new ideology, the use of physical force on behalf of those oppressed or unjustly denied their rights under the old regime becomes legitimate, authorized, and in an important sense conservative. The turning around of society—the rise of the British Parliament, the acquisition of land by the French peasantry, the rise to power of the French bourgeoisie, the seizure of power by the Soviets —came about in the great revolutions by a process that was nearly bloodless. When subsequently much blood was shed, it was as a result of futile attempts either to undo these processes or to carry them further than was to prove feasible. Thus even the events of the great revolutions can be interpreted to sustain the thesis that when the conditions necessary to satisfy the criterion of wastefulness are present, the criterion of gratuitousness usually cannot be satisfied. And when those conditions are not present, the truly admirable course is to remember with Albert Camus that the most profound logic of rebellion is not the logic of destruction but of creation.

Notes

Preface

1. Charles S. Maier, "Mass Hysteria," review of Charles Tilly, Louise Tilly, and Richard Tilly, *The Rebellious Century, 1830–1930* (Cambridge, Mass.: Harvard University Press, 1975), *New Republic*, 2 & 9 August 1975, p. 30.

Introduction

1. Evan Simpson, "Social Norms and Aberrations," *Ethics* 81 (1970): 26–28.
2. Ibid., p. 29.
3. George Rudé, *The Crowd in History*, pp. 254–55.
4. Richard Hofstadter and Michael Wallace, eds., *American Violence*, p. 37.
5. Simpson, pp. 33, 29, 22.
6. Frantz Fanon, *The Wretched of the Earth*, p. 94; Michael Walzer, *Obligations*, p. 67; Robert Moss, *Urban Guerrillas*, p. 28; Irene L. Gendzier, *Frantz Fanon*, pp. 201–2; Kai Nielsen, "Against Moral Conservatism," *Ethics* 82 (1972): **221**.
7. J. L. Austin, *Philosophical Papers*, p. 124. See also J. R. Lucas, *The Freedom of the Will*, pp. 4–9; H. L. A. Hart, *Punishment and Responsibility*, pp. 13–15.
8. Austin, p. 125.
9. Alan A. Silver, "Official Interpretations of Racial Riots," in *Urban Riots*, ed. Robert H. Connery, p. 159. See also E. P. Thompson, "The Moral Economy of the English Crowd in the Eighteenth Century," *Past and Present* 50 (1971): 76–136.

Chapter 1

1. Hofstadter and Wallace, p. 169.
2. Ibid., passim.
3. Wilcomb E. Washburn, *The Governor and the Rebel*.
4. Richard B. Morris, "Insurrection in Massachusetts," in *America in Crisis*, ed. Daniel Aaron, pp. 41–42.
5. Marion L. Starkey, *A Little Rebellion*, p. 133.
6. Leland D. Baldwin, *Whiskey Rebels*, chapter 5; Jacob E. Cooke, "The Whiskey Insurrection," *Pennsylvania History* 30 (1963): 316–46.
7. Quoted in Hugh T. Lefler, *History of North Carolina*, p. 195; Elisha P. Douglass, *Rebels and Democrats*, p. 77.
8. Quoted in John S. Bassett, "The Regulators of North Carolina (1765–1771)," *American Historical Association Annual Meeting*, 1894, p. 152; "Regulator Advertisement, Number Four," 1768, quoted in Lefler, p. 195.
9. Douglass, pp. 78–79, 75.
10. Bassett, p. 154.
11. Douglass, p. 82.
12. Ibid., pp. 85, 86.
13. Ibid., pp. 89, 92–93, 86.
14. Bassett, pp. 189–90; Fanning's official positions included register of deeds, judge of the court, colonel in the militia, and representative to the assembly. Lefler, p. 190; Bassett, pp. 190–91; William S. Powell, James K. Huhta, and Thomas J. Farnham, eds., *The Regulators of North Carolina*, pp. 244–48, 250–55.
15. Elmer D. Johnson, "The War of the Regulation" (M.A. thesis, University of North Carolina, 1942).
16. James Hunter to Maurice Moore, 23 November 1770, in Powell, Huhta, and Farnham, p. 278.
17. Alonso Thomas Dill, *Governor Tryon and His Palace*, p. 147; Bassett, pp. 192, 196.
18. Rednap Howell to James Hunter, quoted in Bassett, p. 198.

19. Council Journal, 18 March 1771, in Powell, Huhta, and Farnham, p. 375.

20. William Tryon to Lord Hillsborough (Secretary of State for the Colonies), 20 October 1770, in Powell, Huhta, and Farnham, p. 273.

21. Powell, Huhta, and Farnham, pp. 359–60, 453.

22. Douglass, pp. 96–97.

23. Mary Elinor Lazenby, *Herman Husband*, p. 111; Caruthers's *Life of Dr. David Caldwell* (1842), cited in Bassett, p. 202; Joseph Seawell Jones, *A Defence of the Revolutionary History of the State of North Carolina from the Aspersions of Mr. Jefferson*, p. 52, citing Francois-Xavier Martin, *History of North Carolina from the Earliest Period* (1829), vol. 2.

24. Bassett, p. 204.

25. Ibid., pp. 208, 209. Quotation p. 208.

26. Eric Foner, ed., *Nat Turner*, p. 1. (Page numbers given in parentheses for Foner refer to this work.)

27. William Styron, *The Confessions of Nat Turner*.

28. George M. Fredrickson and Christopher Lasch, "Resistance to Slavery," *Civil War History* 13 (1967): 318.

29. Vincent Harding, "Religion and Resistance Among Antebellum Negroes, 1800–1860," in *The Making of Black America*, eds. August Meier and Elliott Rudwick, 1:188.

30. John H. Bracey, Jr., August Meier, and Elliott Rudwick, eds., *American Slavery*, pp. 193–94.

31. Foner, pp. 75–76.

32. William W. Freehling, *Prelude to Civil War*, p. 110.

33. Bracey, Meier, and Rudwick, pp. 160–78.

34. Ibid., pp. 176, 175.

35. Philip Taft and Philip Ross, "American Labor Violence," in *Violence in America*, eds. Hugh Davis Graham and Ted Robert Gurr, p. 281.

36. Samuel Yellen, *American Labor Struggles*, p. 73; Henry David, "Upheaval at Homestead," in *America in Crisis*, ed. Daniel Aaron, p. 145; Leon Wolff, *Lockout, The Story of the Homestead Strike of 1892*, p. 74.

37. Wolff, p. 40; David, p. 138. Quotation David, p. 140.

38. David, pp. 138–39.

39. Yellen, p. 77; David, p. 145; Wolff, p. 74.

40. Wolff, p. 80; Yellen, p. 76; David, p. 140.

41. Yellen, p. 81.

42. Ibid., p. 82.

43. Wolff, pp. 95–96.

44. U.S. Congress, House, Committee on the Judiciary, *Labor Troubles at Homestead, Pa.*, 53d Cong., 2d sess., 1893, H. Rept. 2447, pp. 67, 55; cf. Wolff, pp. 96–97.

45. Wolff, pp. 86, 100, 101.

46. Ibid., p. 198; Bernard Hogg, "The Homestead Strike of 1892" (Ph.D. dissertation, University of Chicago, 1943), p. 83.

47. Arthur G. Burgoyne, *Homestead*, p. 59; Hogg, p. 84; cf. Wolff, p. 310; Burgoyne, p. 58; Myron R. Stowell, *"Fort Frick" or the Siege of Homestead*, p. 42; James Howard Bridge, *The Inside History of the Carnegie Steel Company*, p. 213.

48. U.S. Congress, Senate, Select Committee to Investigate the Employment for Private Purposes of Armed Bodies of Men, *Investigation of Labor Troubles*, 53d Cong., 2d sess., 1893, S. Rept. 1280, p. 70.

49. Hogg, p. 84.

50. Ibid., pp. 84–85.

51. Ibid., p. 86; Wolff, p. 114.

52. Hogg, pp. 86–87.

53. Ibid., p. 87.

54. Burgoyne, p. 73.

55. Ibid., p. 72; Hogg, p. 88.

56. Hogg, p. 88.

57. Ibid., p. 90.

58. Ibid.; Burgoyne, p. 81.

59. Hogg, p. 91.

60. Burgoyne, p. 84.

61. Hogg, p. 91.

62. Ibid.; Wolff, p. 128.

63. Burgoyne, pp. 85–86; Wolff, pp. 129–30.

64. Wolff, pp. 110, 112, 116, 121, 128, 130; Burgoyne, pp. 59, 73, 75, 92; Hogg, pp. 94, 139.

65. Wolff, pp. 229, 228.

66. Yellen, p. 94.

67. Wolff, p. 209.

68. Yellen, p. 69.

69. David, p. 169.

70. Ibid., p. 170.

71. Wolff, p. 230. (Page numbers given in parentheses for Wolff refer to this work.) See also Hogg, pp. 173–225, 242–48.

72. Alvin R. Sunseri, "The Ludlow Massacre," *American Chronicle*, January 1972, p. 21; George P. West, *Report on the Colorado Strike*, p. 108.

73. Graham Adams, Jr., *Age of Industrial Violence 1910–15*, pp. 148–51.

74. George S. McGovern and Leonard F. Guttridge, *The Great Coalfield War*, pp. 212–16.

75. Sunseri, p. 23.

76. Ibid., p. 78.

77. Adams, p. 167.

78. Sunseri, p. 24.

79. Ibid., pp. 26, 27.

80. West, p. 124; John A. Fitch, "Law and Order," *Survey* 33 (1914): 256.

81. West, pp. 126, 137.

82. Fitch, p. 257.

83. Adams, p. 138.

84. George S. McGovern, "The Colorado Coal Strike, 1913–1914" (Ph.D. dissertation, Northwestern University, 1953), p. 287.

85. Ibid., p. 292.

86. West, p. 136; Fitch, p. 257.

87. McGovern, pp. 297, 299, 300.

88. McGovern and Guttridge, pp. 263–64.

89. West, pp. 132, 136.

90. Ibid., p. 137; McGovern, p. 305.

91. Austin, p. 125.

92. Adams, p. 172.

93. Yellen, pp. 249–50. The secondary quotation is from B. M. Selekman and M. Van Keeck, *Employes' Representation in Coal Mines: A Study of the Industrial Representation Plan*

of the Colorado Fuel and Iron Company (New York: Russell Sage Foundation, 1924).

Chapter 2

1. G. J. Warnock, *The Object of Morality.* (Page numbers given in parentheses for Warnock refer to this work.)

2. Warnock has conceded that he was mistaken in assimilating obligation to nondeception, but it does not much matter for my use of his argument. See Donald Locke, "The Object of Morality, and the Obligation to Keep a Promise," *Canadian Journal of Philosophy* 2 (1972–73): 135–43; G. J. Warnock, "Comment on Locke," ibid., pp. 389–90.

3. John Rawls, *A Theory of Justice,* p. 109.

4. *Report of the Colorado Strike* (Washington, D.C.: U.S. Commission of Industrial Relations, 1915), p. 135.

5. Warnock, pp. 81–82.

6. Ibid., p. 83.

7. *Nation,* 28 July 1892, cited in Wolff, p. 199.

8. Sanford Levinson, "Responsibility for Crimes of War," *Philosophy and Public Affairs* 2 (1973): 244–73.

9. Warnock, pp. 116, 117 (but see note 2).

10. Eugene Genovese, "American Slaves and Their History," *New York Review of Books,* 3 December 1970, pp. 39, 40.

11. Quoted by Gerry Mullin, "Religion, Acculturation, and American Negro Slave Rebellions," in Bracey, Meier, and Rudwick, p. 166.

12. H. L. A. Hart, "Are There Any Natural Rights?," *Philosophical Review* 64 (1955): 185.

13. For a defense of these presuppositions, see Hart, "Are There Any Natural Rights?," and Ronald Dworkin, *Taking Rights Seriously,* chapter 7. Quotation from Dworkin, p. 188.

14. Kenneth M. Stampp, *The Peculiar Institution,* pp. 292, 294.

15. W. E. B. DuBois, *Black Reconstruction in America* (New York, 1962) pp. 8–9, quoted in Eugene D. Genovese, *Roll, Jordan, Roll,* p. 69; Genovese, *Roll, Jordan, Roll,* p. 88.

16. Genovese, *Roll, Jordan, Roll,* pp. 4, 5, 6–7. (Page num-

bers given in parentheses for Genovese refer to this work.)

17. Burgoyne, pp. 59, 92; cf. Joseph Frazier Wall, *Andrew Carnegie*, p. 559.

18. Lawrence H. Tribe, "Policy Science," *Philosophy and Public Affairs* 2 (1972): 82, 83.

Chapter 3

1. American Law Institute, *Model Penal Code*, Tentative Draft No. 8. (Page numbers given in parentheses for the *Model Penal Code* [*MPC*] refer to this work.)

2. Baruch Brody, "Thomson on Abortion," *Philosophy and Public Affairs* 1 (1972): 335.

3. *Model Penal Code*, p. 24, quoting Beale, "Retreat from Murderous Assault," *Harvard Law Review* 16 (1903): 581.

4. Levinson, p. 245.

5. Peter L. Berger and Richard John Neuhaus, *Movement and Revolution*, pp. 160–63.

6. Robert Forster and Jack P. Greene, eds., *Preconditions of Revolution in Early Modern Europe*, pp. 1, 57; John Dunn, *Modern Revolutions*, pp. 12, 228–29.

7. W. G. Runciman, "Explaining Social Stratification," in *Imagination and Precision in the Social Sciences*, eds. T. J. Nossiter, A. H. Hanson, and Stein Rokkan, p. 169.

8. Eugene D. Genovese, *The Political Economy of Slavery*, p. 29.

9. Barron B. Beshoar, *Out of the Depths*, pp. xi, 162.

10. H. Stuart Hughes, "A Historian's Critique of Violence from the French Revolution to Vietnam," in *Perspectives on Violence,* ed. Gene Usdin, pp. 17–29.

11. Dunn, p. 237.

12. Berger and Neuhaus, p. 160.

Chapter 4

1. Rawls, *A Theory of Justice*. (Page numbers given in parentheses for Rawls refer to this work.)

2. Ronald Dworkin, *Taking Rights Seriously*, chapter 6.

3. Ibid., especially pp. 177–83.

4. A. J. Richards, *A Theory of Reasons for Actions*, pp. 177, 121, 151, 157.

5. Robert A. Dahl, *After the Revolution?*; Walter Dean Burnham, "The Changing Shape of the American Political Universe," *American Political Science Review* 59 (1965): 7–28; Lester Thurow, "Toward a Definition of Economic Justice," *Public Interest*, Spring 1973, pp. 56–80; cf. Michael Walzer, "A Day in the Life of a Socialist Citizen," *Dissent*, May–June 1968, pp. 243–47.

6. Rawls, pp. 372–73.

7. Antony Flew, "Ends and Means," *Encyclopedia of Philosophy*, p. 510.

8. Ibid.

9. J. M. Cameron, "On Violence," *New York Review of Books*, 2 July 1970, p. 30.

10. Hofstadter and Wallace, p. 38.

11. Rudé, pp. 256, 94; M. J. Sydenham, *The French Revolution*, p. 111.

12. William Henry Chamberlain, *The Russian Revolution*, 1: 313, 341.

13. Ted Honderich, "Democratic Violence," *Philosophy and Public Affairs* 2 (1973): 208, 212.

14. Don Higginbotham, *The War of American Independence*, pp. 94, 362, 375.

15. Donald Greer, *The Incidence of the Terror During the French Revolution*, chapter 2; Michael Walzer, ed., *Regicide and Revolution*, p. 87.

16. Lazar Volin, *A Century of Russian Agriculture*, pp. 148–50; Christopher Hill, *Lenin and the Russian Revolution*, pp. 134–35.

17. Michael Walzer, "Moral Judgment in Time of War," in *War and Morality*, ed. Richard A. Wasserstrom, p. 60.

18. Gerald C. MacCallum, Jr., "Reform, Violence, and Personal Integrity," *Inquiry* 14 (1971): 308; Rawls, p. 373.

19. MacCallum, p. 308, 307.

20. Ibid., p. 308; Rawls, p. 376.

21. Raul Hilberg, *The Destruction of the European Jewry*, p. 322; Lucy S. Dawidowicz, *The War Against the Jews*, pp. 300–310.

22. Hilberg, pp. 323, 326; Dawidowicz, pp. 336–40.

23. Isaiah Trunk, *Judenrat*, pp. 452, 463–67.

24. Dawidowicz, pp. 313, 338, 313–14, 314.

25. Michael Walzer, "The Memory of Justice," *New Republic*, 9 October 1976, p. 22.

26. Ibid., p. 23.

27. Dawidowicz, p. 318.

28. MacCallum, p. 307.

29. Genovese, *Roll, Jordan, Roll*, p. 588.

30. Elizabeth Anscombe, "War and Murder," in Wasserstrom, pp. 42–53. (Page numbers given in parentheses for Anscombe refer to this article.) "War and Murder" was originally published in *Nuclear Weapons: A Catholic Response*, ed. Walter Stein (New York: Sheed and Ward, 1961), pp. 45–62.

31. Thomas Nagel, "War and Massacre," *Philosophy and Public Affairs* 1 (1972): 139.

32. Philippa Foot, "Abortion and the Doctrine of the Double Effect," in *An Introduction to Moral and Social Philosophy*, ed. Jeffrie G. Murphy, pp. 384–94. (Numbers given in parentheses for Foot refer to this article as it appears in Murphy.) Foot's article was first published in *Oxford Review* 5 (1967).

33. Hofstadter and Wallace, p. 199.

34. Rudé, pp. 19–191.

35. Ibid., pp. 156–63.

36. Hofstadter and Wallace, p. 38.

37. Ibid., p. 30.

Works Cited

Adams, Graham, Jr. *Age of Industrial Violence 1910–15: The Activities and Findings of the United States Commission on Industrial Relations.* New York: Columbia University Press, 1966.

American Law Institute. *Model Penal Code* (Tentative Draft No. 8). Philadelphia: American Law Institute, 1958.

Anscombe, Elizabeth. "War and Murder." In *War and Morality,* edited by Richard A. Wasserstrom. Belmont, Calif.: Wadsworth, 1970.

Austin, J. L. *Philosophical Papers.* Oxford: Clarendon Press, 1961.

Baldwin, Leland D. *Whiskey Rebels: The Story of a Frontier Uprising.* Pittsburgh: University of Pittsburgh Press, 1939.

Bassett, John S. "The Regulators of North Carolina (1765–1771)." *American Historical Association Annual Meeting,* 1894, pp. 141–212.

Berger, Peter L., and Neuhaus, Richard John. *Movement and Revolution.* Garden City, N. Y.: Doubleday, 1970.

Beshoar, Barron B. *Out of the Depths: The Story of John R. Lawson a Labor Leader.* Denver: Colorado Labor Historical Committee of the Denver Trades and Labor Assembly, 1942.

Bridge, James Howard. *The Inside History of the Carnegie Steel Company: A Romance of Millions.* New York: Aldine, 1903.

Brody, Baruch. "Thomson on Abortion." *Philosophy and Public Affairs* 1 (1972): 335–40.

Burgoyne, Arthur G. *Homestead: A Complete History of the Struggle of July, 1892, between the Carnegie Steel Company, Limited, and the Amalgamated Association of Iron and Steel*

Workers. Pittsburgh: Rawsthorne Engraving and Printing Co.. 1893.

Burnham, Walter Dean. "The Changing Shape of the American Political Universe." *American Political Science Review* 59 (1965): 7–28.

Cameron, J. M. "A Special Supplement: On Violence." *New York Review of Books*, 2 July 1970, pp. 24–32.

Chamberlain, William Henry. *The Russian Revolution: 1917–1921*. 2 vols. New York: Grosset and Dunlap, 1965.

Cooke, Jacob E. "The Whiskey Insurrection: A Re-Evaluation." *Pennsylvania History* 30 (1963): 216–46.

Dahl, Robert A. *After the Revolution? Authority in A Good Society*. New Haven: Yale University Press, 1970.

David, Henry. "Upheaval at Homestead." In *America in Crisis: Fourteen Crucial Episodes in American History*, edited by Daniel Aaron. New York: Knopf, 1952.

Dawidowicz, Lucy. *The War Against the Jews, 1933–1945*. New York: Holt, Rinehart and Winston, 1975.

Dill, Alonzo Thomas. *Governor Tryon and His Palace*. Chapel Hill: University of North Carolina Press, 1955.

Douglas, Elisha P. *Rebels and Democrats: The Struggle for Equal Political Rights and Majority Rule During the American Revolution*. Chapel Hill: University of North Carolina Press, 1955.

Dunn, John. *Modern Revolutions: An Introduction to the Analysis of a Political Phenomenon*. Cambridge: Cambridge University Press, 1972.

Dworkin, Ronald. *Taking Rights Seriously*. Cambridge, Mass.: Harvard University Press, 1977.

Fanon, Frantz. *The Wretched of the Earth*. Translated by Constance Farrington. New York: Grove Press, 1968.

Fitch, John A. "Law and Order: The Issue in Colorado." *Survey* 33 (1914): 241–58.

Flew, Antony. "Ends and Means." *Encyclopedia of Philosophy*, edited by Paul Edwards. New York: Macmillan and Free Press, 1967.

Foner, Eric, ed., *Nat Turner*. Englewood Cliffs, N. J.: Prentice-Hall, 1971.

Foot, Philippa. "Abortion and the Doctrine of Double Effect." In *An Introduction to Moral and Social Philosophy: Basic Readings in Theory and Practice*, edited by Jeffrie G. Murphy. Belmont, Calif.: Wadsworth, 1973.

Foster, Robert, and Greene, Jack P., eds., *Preconditions of Revolution in Early Modern Europe*. Baltimore: Johns Hopkins Press, 1970.

Fredrickson, George M., and Lasch, Christopher. "Resistance to Slavery." *Civil War History* 13 (1967): 315–29.

Freehling, William W. *Prelude to Civil War: The Nullification Controversy in South Carolina, 1816–1836*. New York: Harper Torchbooks, 1965.

Gendzier, Irene L. *Frantz Fanon: A Critical Study*. New York: Pantheon, 1973.

Genovese, Eugene D. "American Slaves and Their History." *New York Review of Books*, 3 December 1970, pp. 38–44.

———. *The Political Economy of Slavery: Studies in the Economy and Society of the Slave South*. New York: Random House, 1967.

———. *Roll, Jordan, Roll: The World the Slaves Made*. New York: Random House, 1974.

Greer, Donald. *The Incidence of the Terror During the French Revolution*. Cambridge: Harvard University Press, 1935.

Harding, Vincent. "Religion and Resistance Among Antebellum Negroes, 1800–1860." In *The Making of Black America: Essays in Negro Life and History*, edited by August Meier and Elliott Rudwick. Vol. 1. New York: Atheneum, 1969.

Hart, H. L. A. "Are There Any Natural Rights?" *Philosophical Review* 64 (1955): 175–91.

———. *Punishment and Responsibility: Essays in the Philosophy of Law*. New York: Oxford University Press, 1968.

Higginbotham, Don. *The War of American Independence: Military Attitudes, Policies, and Practice, 1763–1789*. New York: Macmillan, 1971.

Hilberg, Raul. *The Destruction of the European Jews*. Chicago: Quadrangle Books, 1961.

Hill, Christopher. *Lenin and the Russian Revolution*. Middlesex, England: Penguin, 1971.

Hofstadter, Richard, and Wallace, Michael, eds. *American Violence: A Documentary History*. New York: Knopf, 1970.

Hogg, J. Bernard. "The Homestead Strike of 1892." Ph.D. dissertation, University of Chicago, 1943.

Honderich, Ted. "Democratic Violence." *Philosophy and Public·Affairs* 2 (1973): 190–214.

Hughes, H. Stuart. "A Historian's Critique of Violence from the French Revolution to Vietnam." In *Perspectives on Violence*, edited by Gene Usdin. New York: Brunner Mazel, 1972.

Johnson, Elmer D. "The War of the Regulation: Its Place in History." M.A. thesis, University of North Carolina, 1942.

Jones, Joseph Seawell. *A Defense of the Revolutionary History of the State of North Carolina from the Aspersions of Mr. Jefferson*. Boston: Charles Bowen, 1834.

Lazenby, Mary Elinor. *Herman Husband: A Story of His Life*. Washington, D.C.: Old Neighborhoods Press, 1940.

Lefler, Hugh T. *History of North Carolina*. New York: Lewis Historical Publishing Co., 1956.

Levinson, Sanford. "Responsibility for Crimes of War." *Philosophy and Public Affairs* 2 (1973): 244–73.

Locke, Donald. "The Object of Morality, and the Obligation to Keep a Promise." *Canadian Journal of Philosophy* 2 (1972–73): 135–43.

Lucas, J. R. *The Freedom of the Will*. Oxford: Clarendon Press, 1970.

MacCallum, Gerald C., Jr. "Reform, Violence, and Personal Integrity: A Commentary on the Saying That You Ought to Fight for What You Believe Right." *Inquiry* 14 (1971): 301–17.

McGovern, George S. "The Colorado Coal Strike, 1913–1914." Ph.D. dissertation, Northwestern University, 1953.

McGovern, George S., and Guttridge, Leonard F. *The Great Coalfield War*. Boston: Houghton Mifflin, 1972.

Morris, Richard. "Insurrection in Massachusetts." In *America in Crisis: Fourteen Crucial Episodes in American History*, edited by Daniel Aaron. New York: Knopf, 1952.

Moss, Robert. *Urban Guerrillas: The New Face of Political Violence*. London: Temple Smith, 1972.

Mullin, Gerry. "Religion, Acculturation, and American Negro Slave Rebellions: Gabriel's Insurrection." In *American Slavery: The Question of Resistance*, edited by John H. Bracey, Jr., August Meier, and Elliott Rudwick. Belmont, Calif.: Wadsworth, 1971.

Nagel, Thomas. "War and Massacre." *Philosophy and Public Affairs* 1 (1972): 123–44.

Nielsen, Kai. "Against Moral Conservatism." *Ethics* 82 (1972): 219–31.

Patterson, H. Orlando. "The General Causes of Jamaican Slave Revolts." In *American Slavery: The Question of Resistance*, edited by John H. Bracey, Jr., August Meier, and Elliott Rudwick. Belmont, Calif.: Wadsworth, 1971.

Powell, William S.; Huhta, James K.; and Farnham, Thomas J., eds. *The Regulators in North Carolina: A Documentary History 1759–1776*. Raleigh, N. C.: State Department of Archives and History, 1971.

Rawls, John. *A Theory of Justice*. Cambridge, Mass.: Belknap Press, 1971.

Richards, David A. J. *A Theory of Reasons for Action*. Oxford: Clarendon Press, 1971.

Rudé, George. *The Crowd in History: A Study of Popular Disturbances in France and England 1730–1848*. New York: Wiley, 1964.

Runciman, W. G. "Explaining Social Stratification." In *Imagination and Precision in the Social Sciences*, edited by T. J. Nossiter, A. H. Hanson, and Stein Rokkan. London: Faber and Faber, 1972.

Silver, Allan A. "Official Interpretations of Racial Riots." In *Urban Riots: Violence and Social Change*, edited by Robert Connery. New York: Random House, 1968.

Simpson, Evan. "Social Norms and Aberrations: Violence and Some Related Social Facts." *Ethics* 81 (1970): 22–35.

Stampp, Kenneth M. *The Peculiar Institution: Slavery in the Ante-Bellum South*. New York: Random House, 1956.

Starkey, Marion L. *A Little Rebellion*. New York: Knopf, 1955.

Stowell, Myron R. *"Fort Frick"; or, The Siege of Homestead: A History of the Famous Struggle between the Amalgamated Association of Iron and Steel Workers and the Carnegie Steel Company (Limited) of Pittsburgh, Pa.* Pittsburgh: Pittsburgh Printing Co., 1893.

Styron, William. *The Confessions of Nat Turner*. New York: Signet, 1966.

Sunseri, Alvin R. "The Ludlow Massacre: A Study in the Mis-Employment of the National Guard." *American Chronicle: A Magazine of History*, January 1972, pp. 21–28.

Sydenham, M. J. *The French Revolution*. London: Botsford, 1965.

Taft, Philip, and Russ, Philip. "American Labor Violence: Its Causes, Character, and Outcome." In *The History of Violence in America: Historical and Comparative Perspectives*, edited by Hugh Davis Graham and Ted Robert Gurr. New York: Praeger, 1969.

Thompson, E. P. "The Moral Economy of the English Crowd in the Eighteenth Century." *Past and Present* 50 (1971): 76–136.

Thurow, Lester. "Toward a Definition of Economic Justice." *Public Interest*, Spring 1973, pp. 56–80.

Tribe, Lawrence H. "Policy Science: Analysis or Ideology?" *Philosophy and Public Affairs* 2 (1972): 66–110.

Trunk, Isaiah. *Judenrat: The Jewish Councils in Eastern Europe Under Nazi Occupation*. New York: Macmillan, 1972.

U.S., Congress, House, Committee on the Judiciary. *Labor Troubles at Homestead, Pa.* 53d Cong., 2d sess., 1893, H. Rept. 2447.

U.S., Congress, Senate, Select Committee To Investigate the Employment for Private Purposes of Armed Bodies of Men. *Investigation of Labor Troubles*. 53d Cong., 2d sess., 1893, S. Rept. 1280.

Volin, Lazar. *A Century of Russian Agriculture: From Alexander II to Khrushchev*. Cambridge, Mass.: Harvard University Press, 1970.

Wall, Joseph Frazier. *Andrew Carnegie*. New York: Oxford University Press, 1970.

Walzer, Michael. "A Day in the Life of the Socialist Citizen." *Dissent* May–June 1968, pp. 243–47.

———. "The Memory of Justice." *New Republic*, 9 October 1976, pp. 19–23.

———. "Moral Judgment in Time of War." *War and Morality*, edited by Richard A. Wasserstrom. Belmont, Calif.: Wadsworth, 1970, pp. 54–62.

———. *Obligations: Essays on Disobedience, War, and Citizenship*. Cambridge, Mass.: Harvard University Press, 1970.

———, ed. *Regicide and Revolution: Speeches at the Trial of Louis XVI*. Translated by Marian Rothestein. Cambridge: Cambridge University Press, 1974.

Warnock, G. J. "Comment on Locke." *Canadian Journal of Philosophy* 2 (1972–73): 389–90.

———. *The Object of Morality*. London: Methuen, 1971.

Washburn, Wilcomb E. *The Governor and the Rebel: A History of Bacon's Rebellion in Virginia*. Chapel Hill: University of North Carolina Press, 1957.

Wasserstrom, Richard A. "On the Morality of War: A Preliminary Inquiry." In *War and Morality*, edited by Richard A. Wasserstrom. Belmont, Calif.: Wadsworth, 1970.

West, George P. *Report on the Colorado Strike*. Washington, D.C.: U.S. Commission on Industrial Relations, 1915.

Wolff, Leon. *Lockout, The Story of the Homestead Strike of 1892: A Study of Violence, Unionism, and the Carnegie Steel Empire*. New York: Harper and Row, 1965.

Yellen, Samuel. *American Labor Struggles*. New York: Russell, 1936.

Index